THE PICTURE BOOK OF

ANIMAL FRIENDS

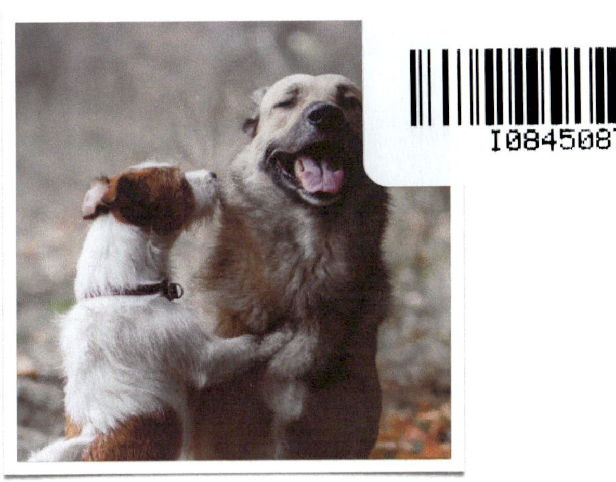

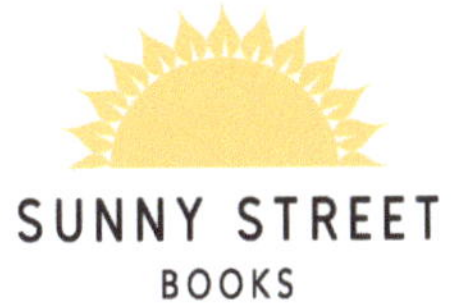

SUNNY STREET
BOOKS

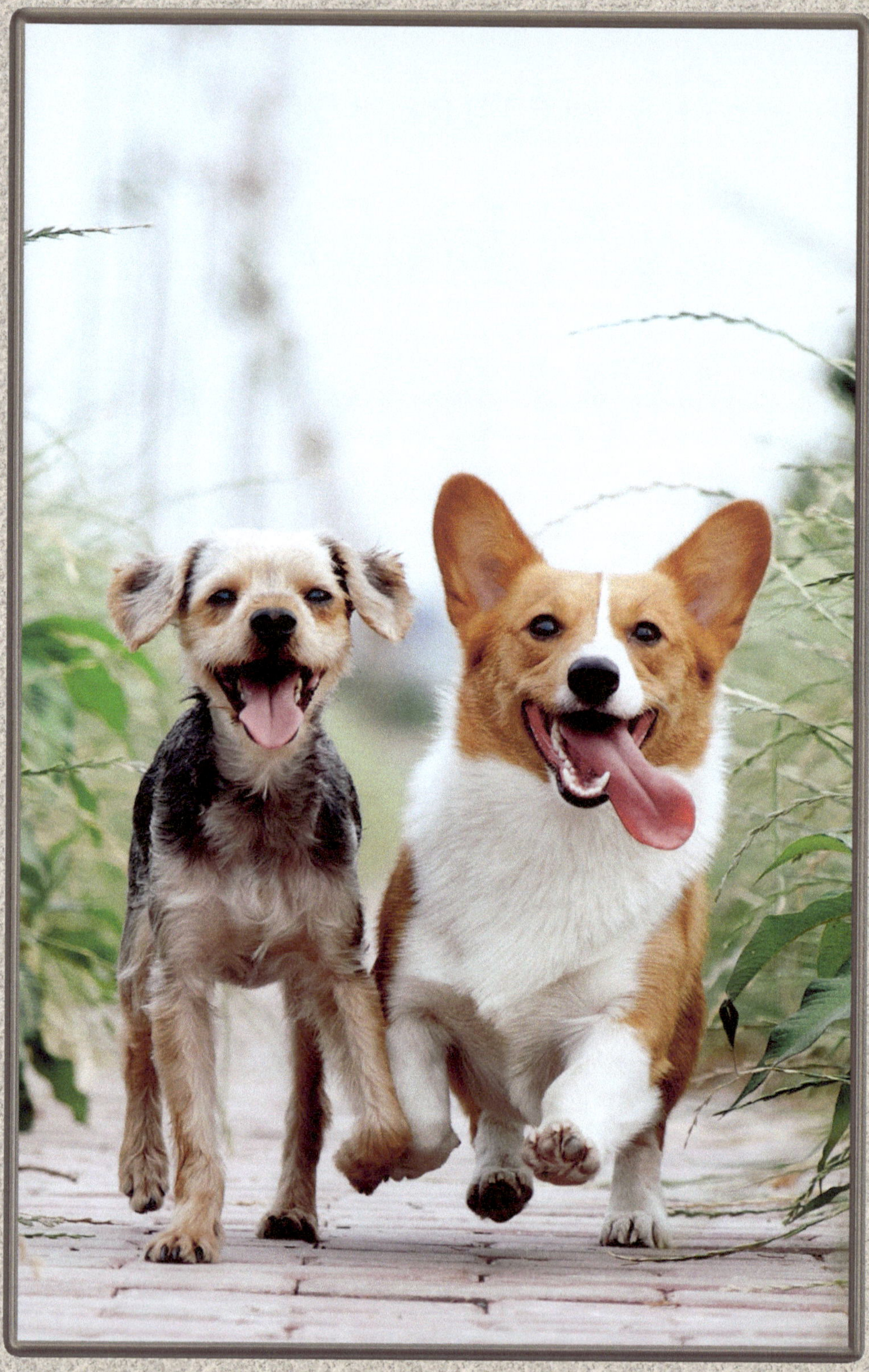

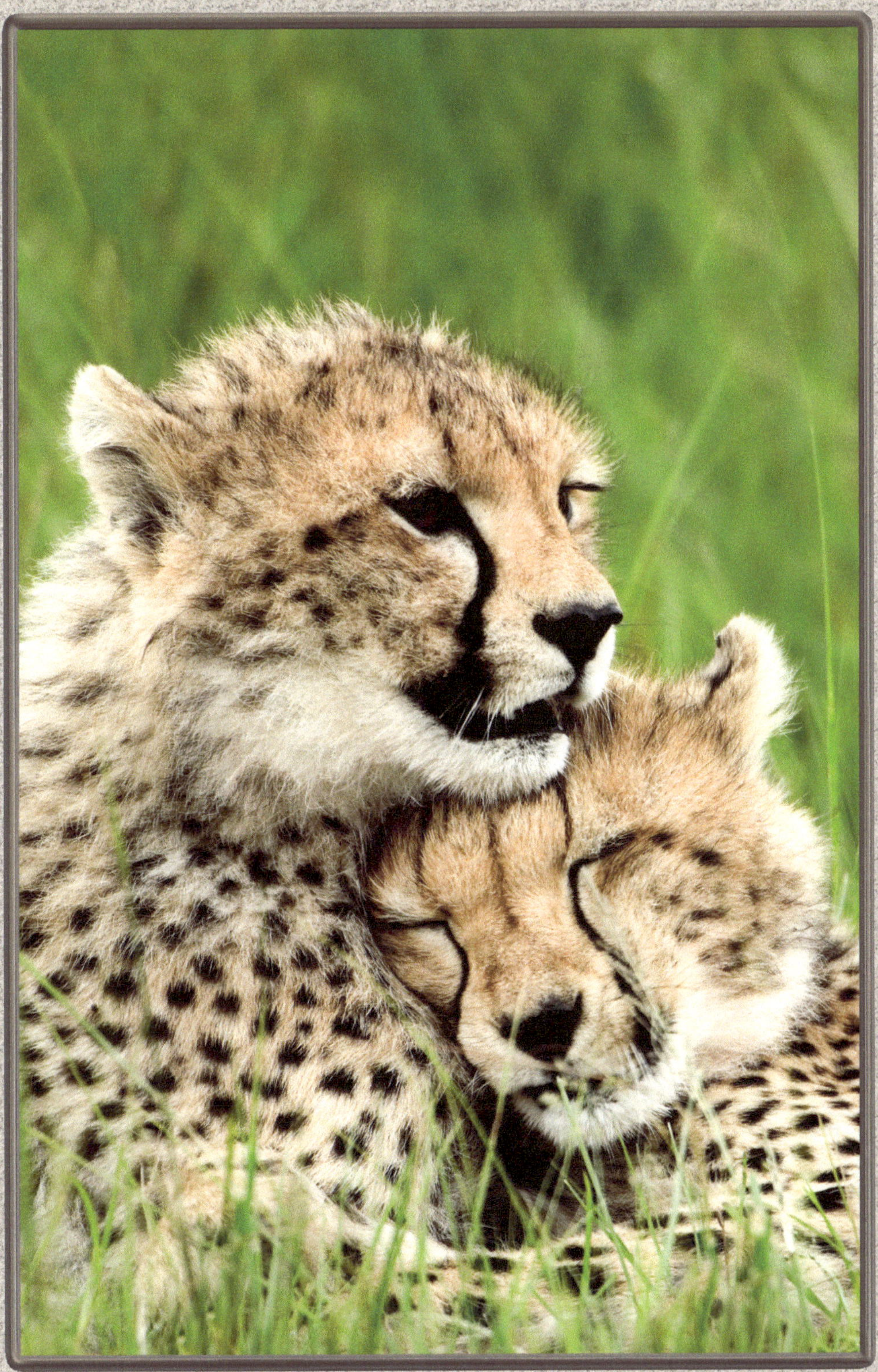

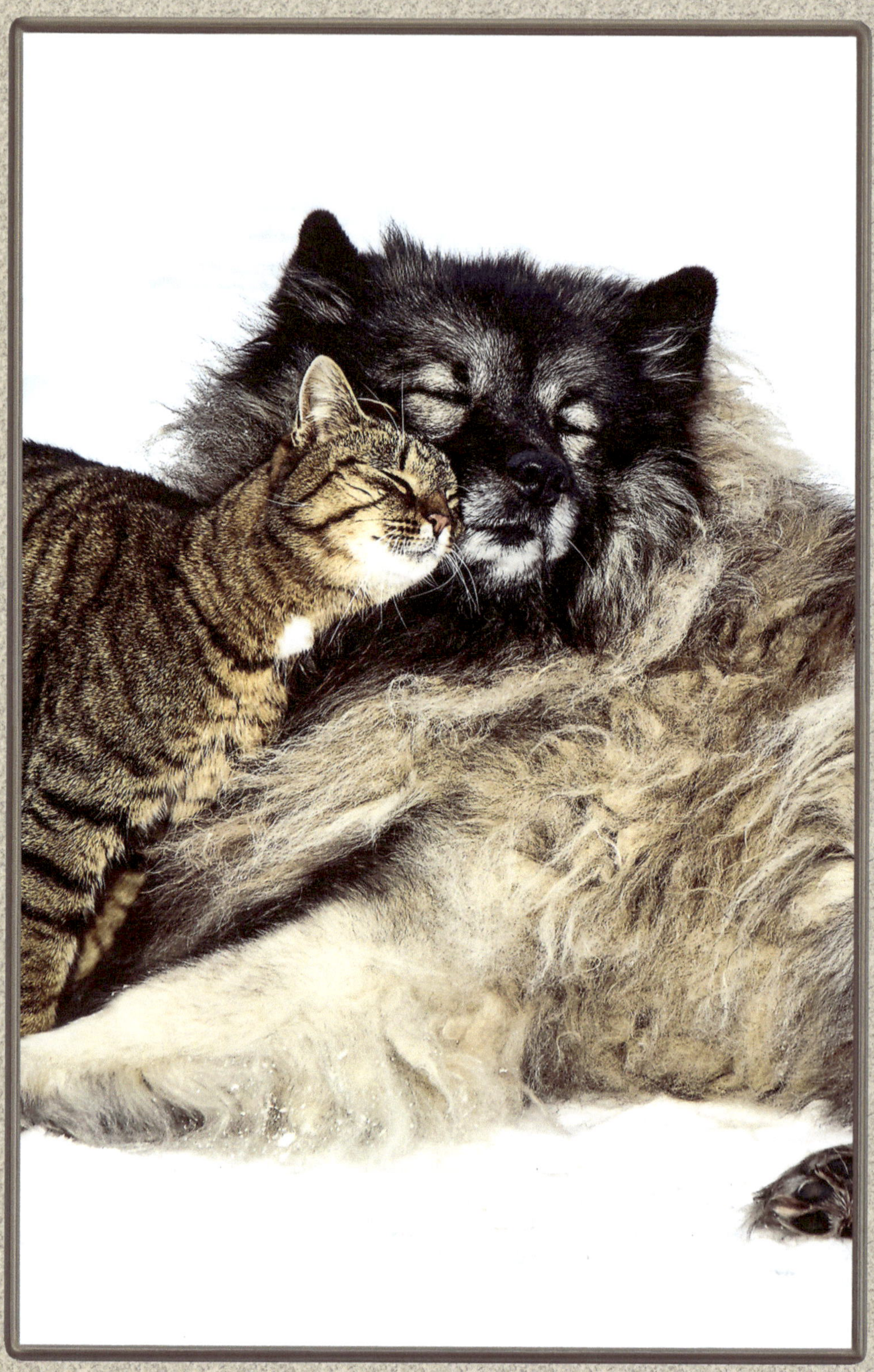

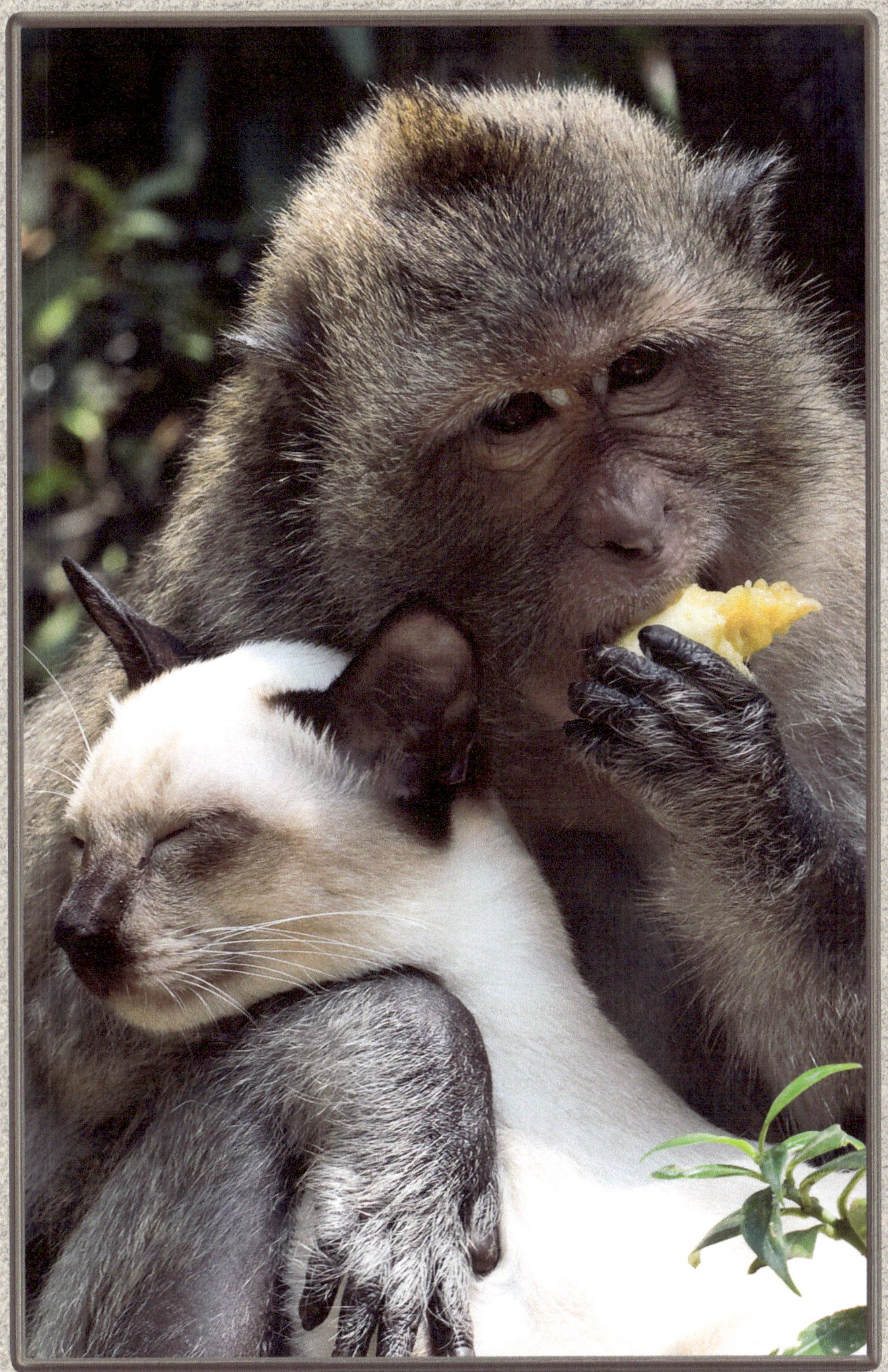

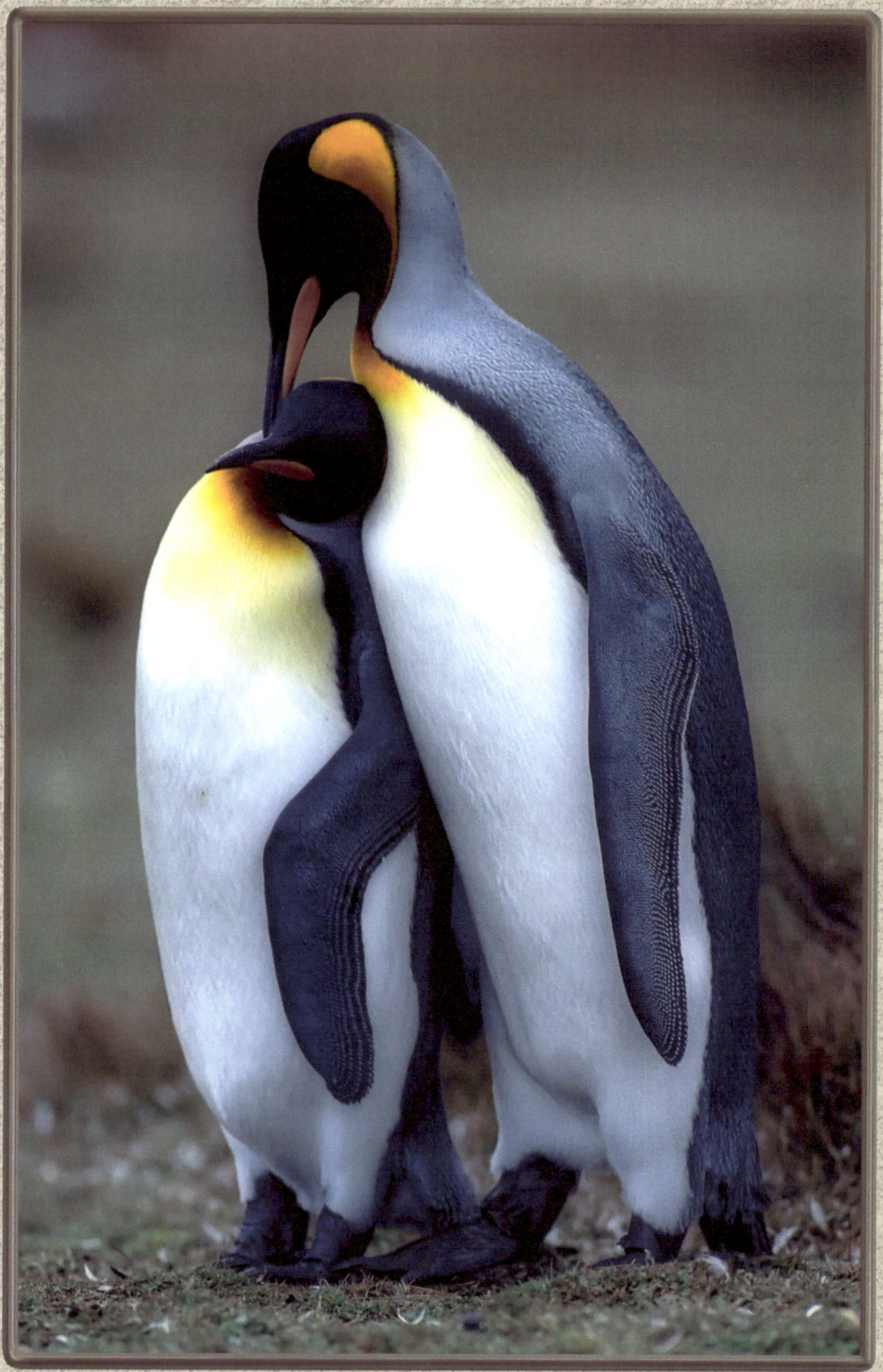

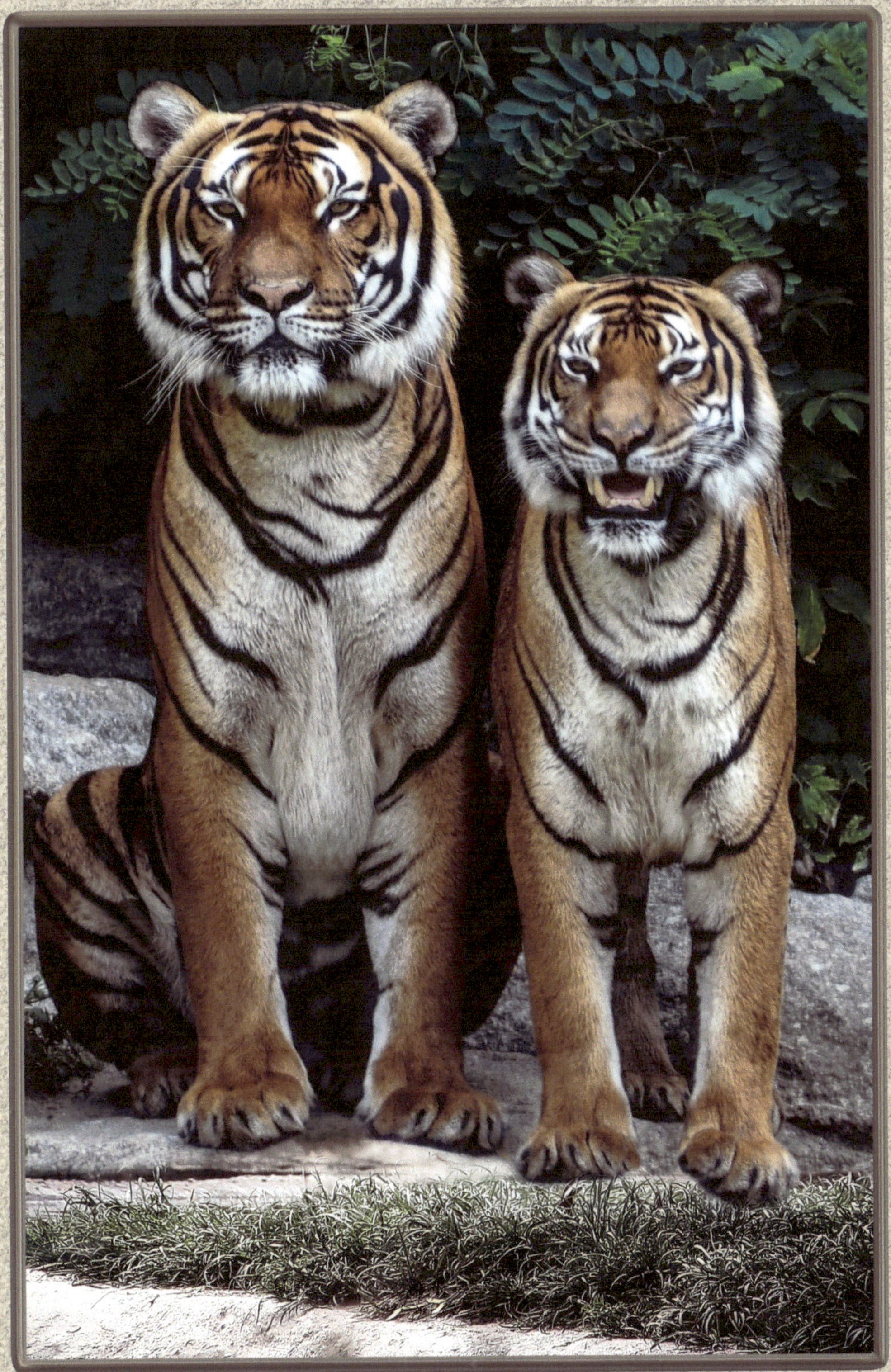

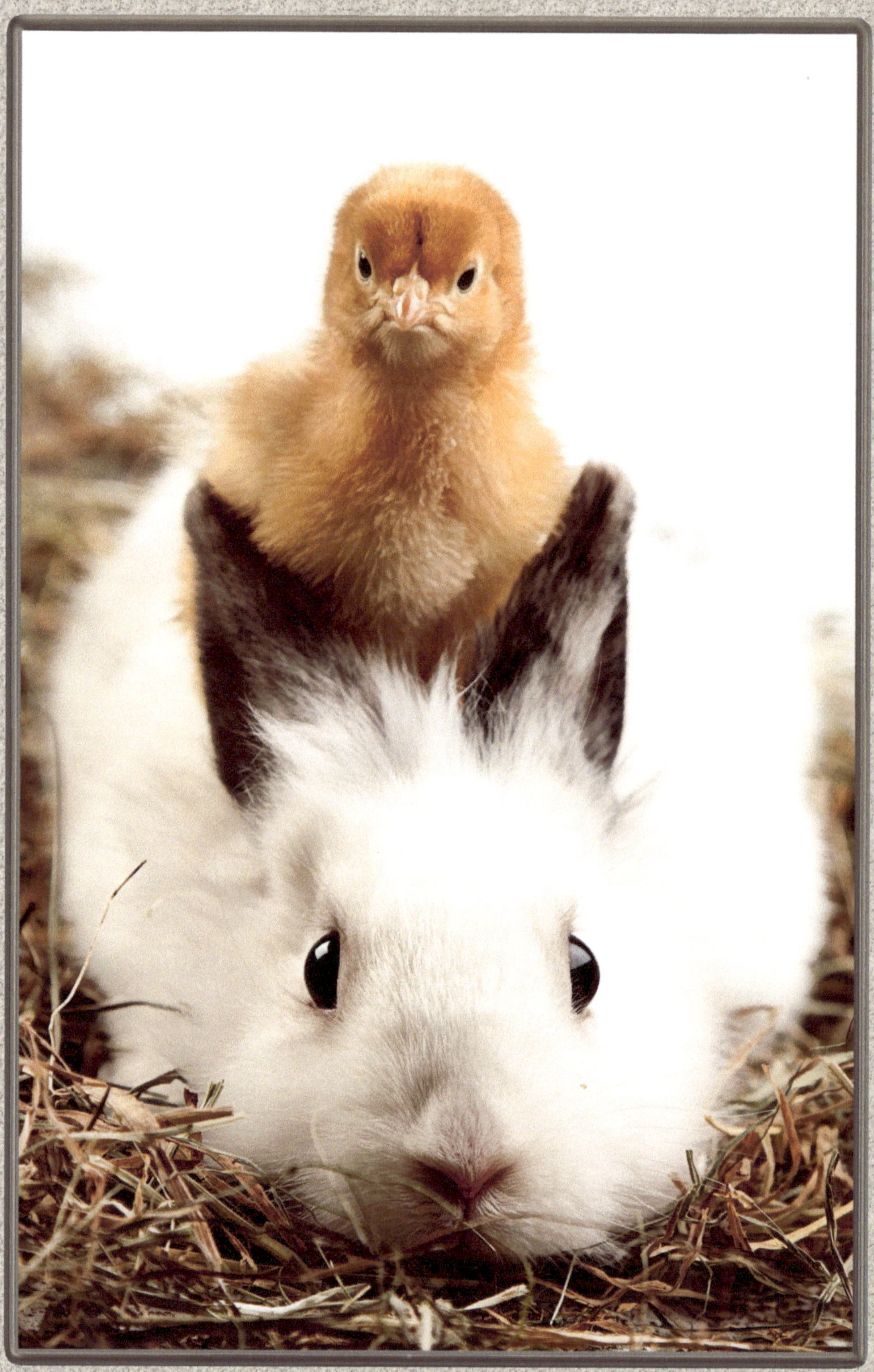

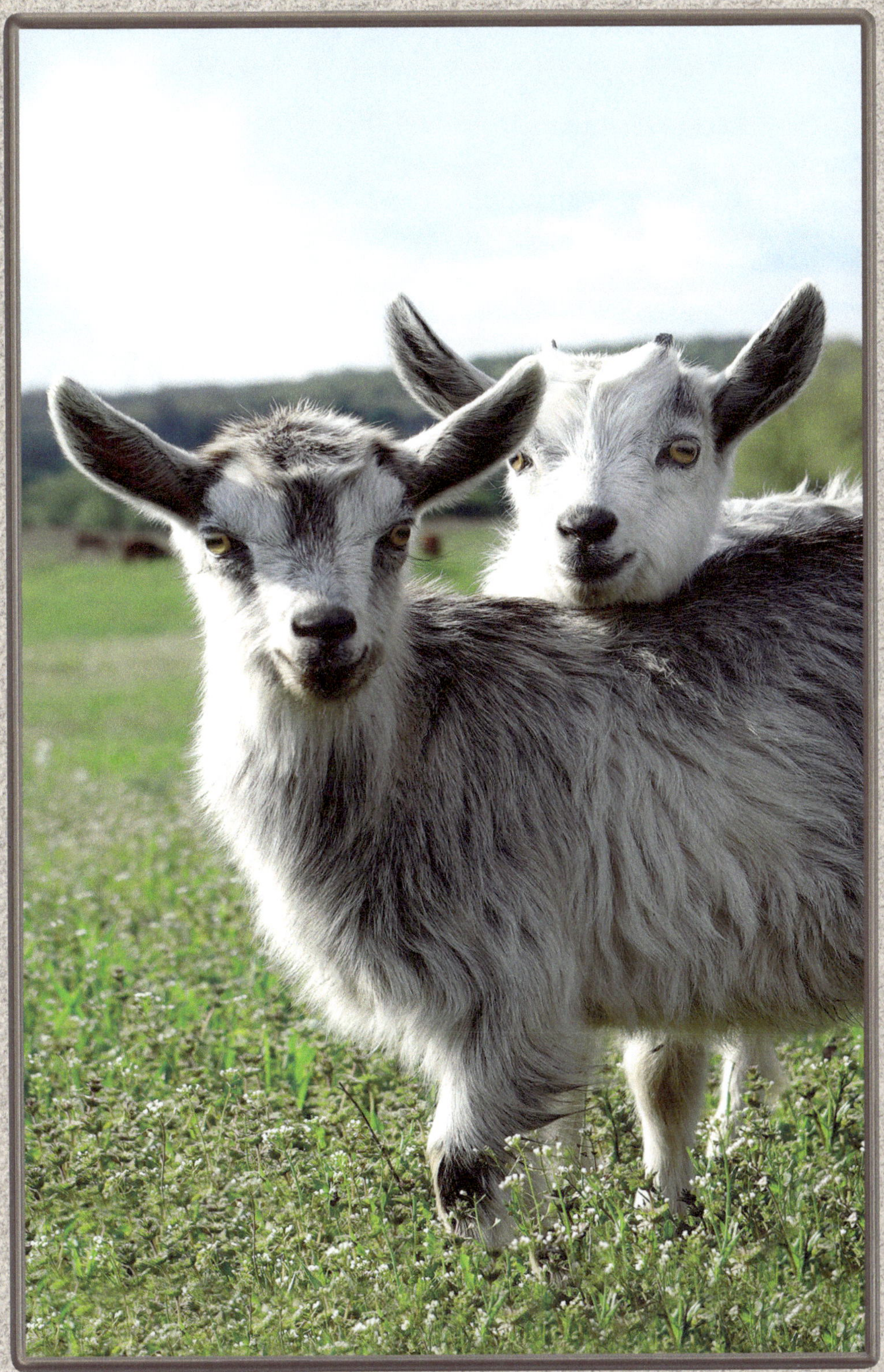

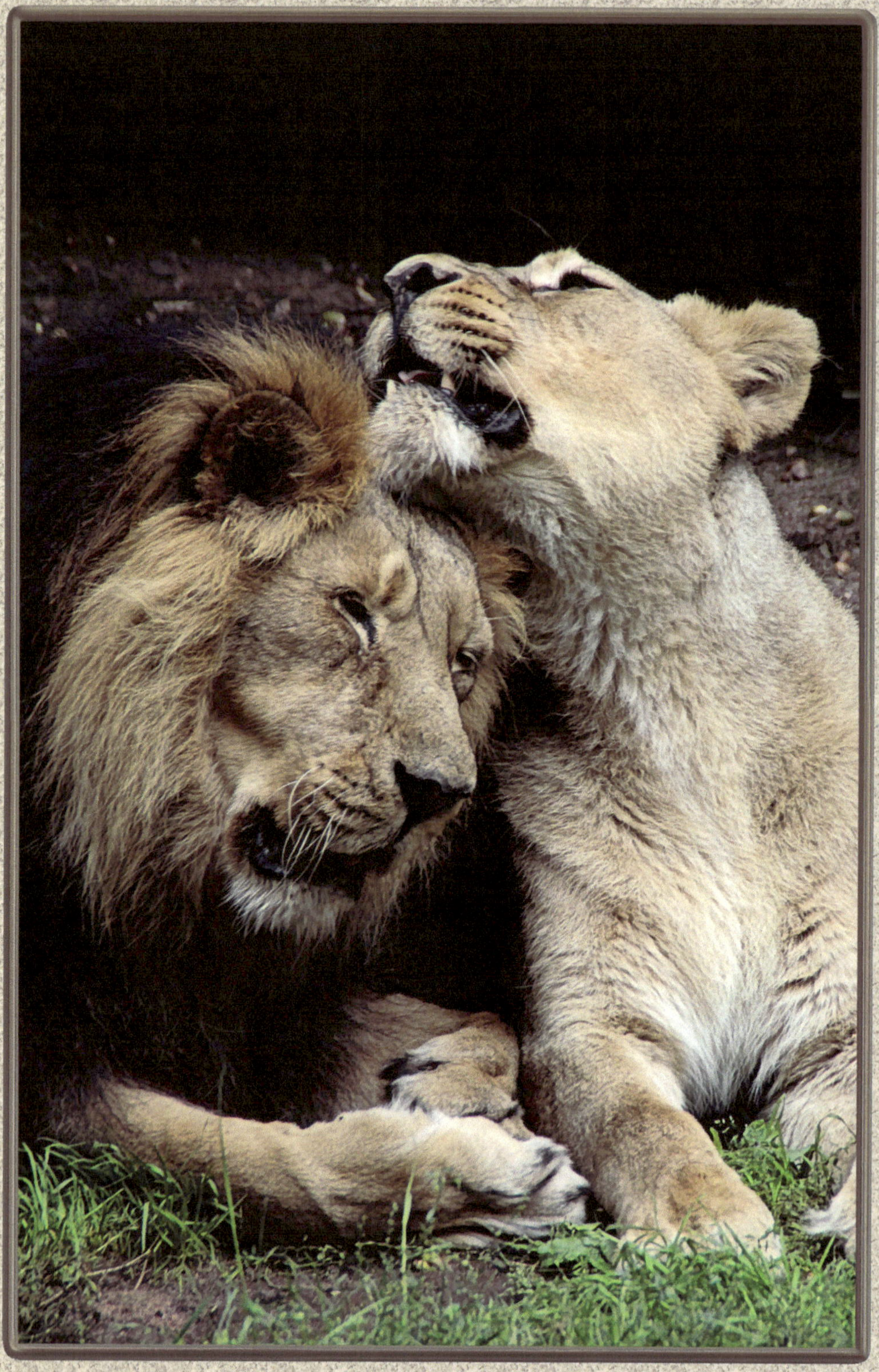

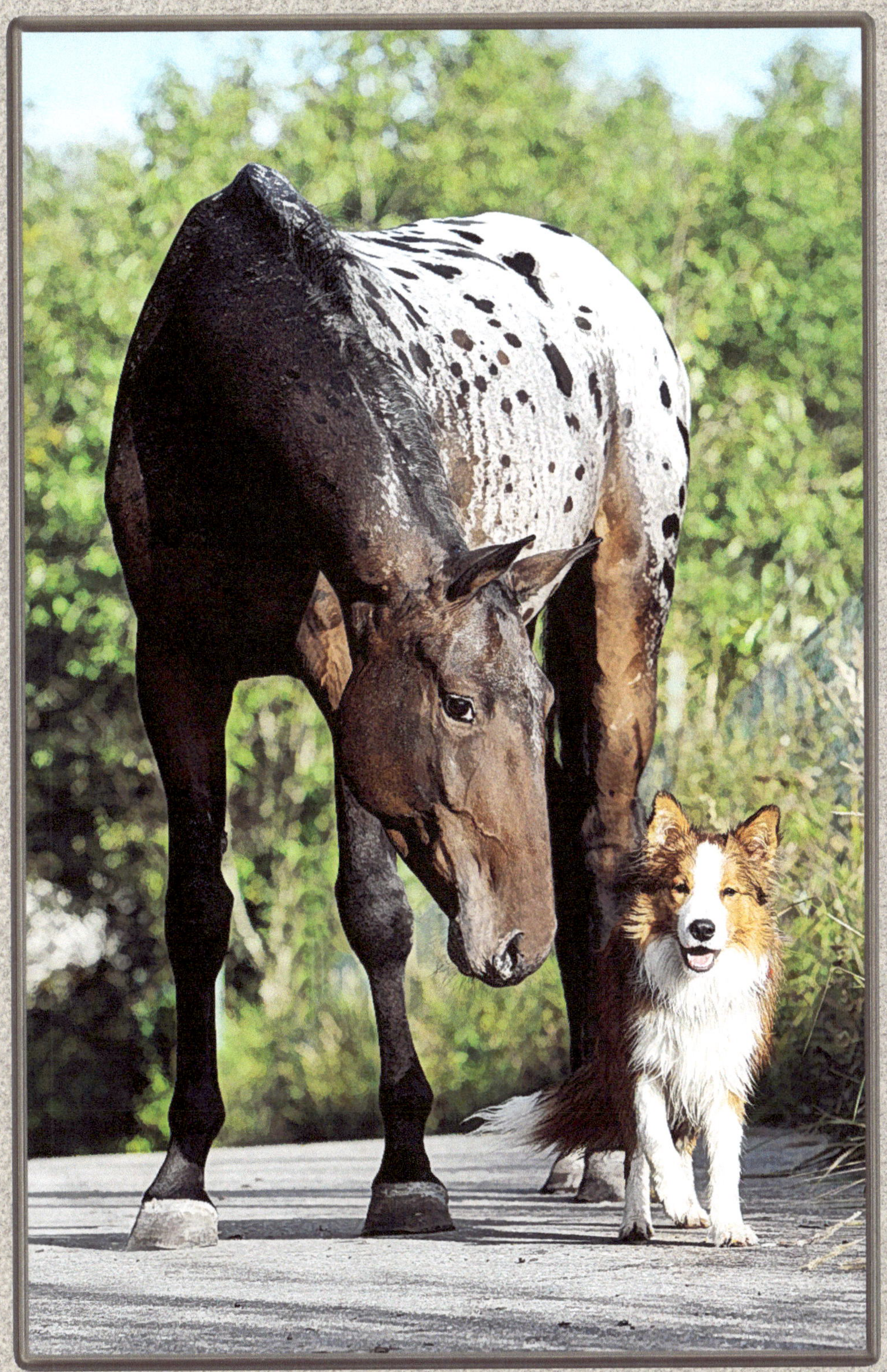

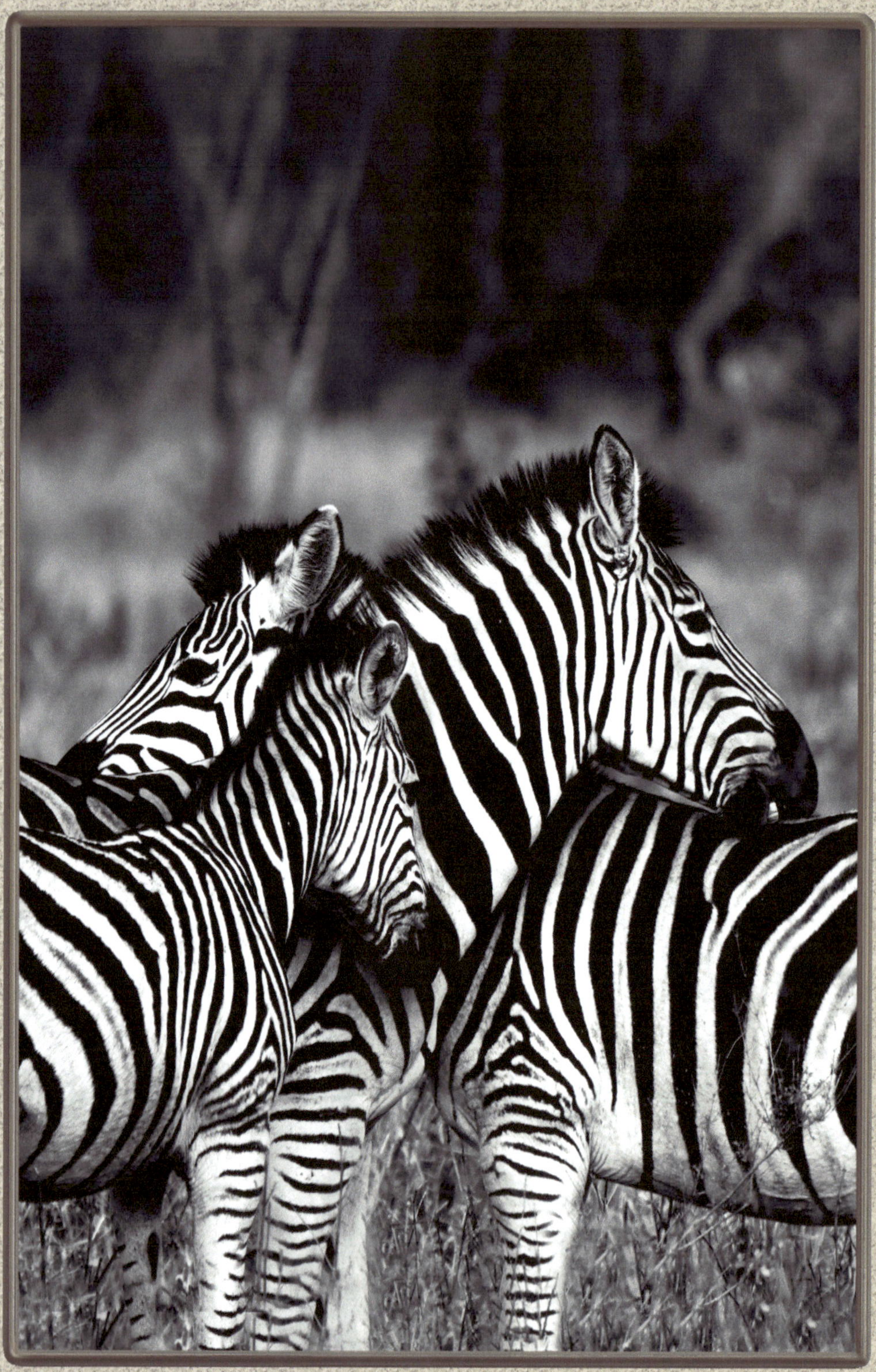

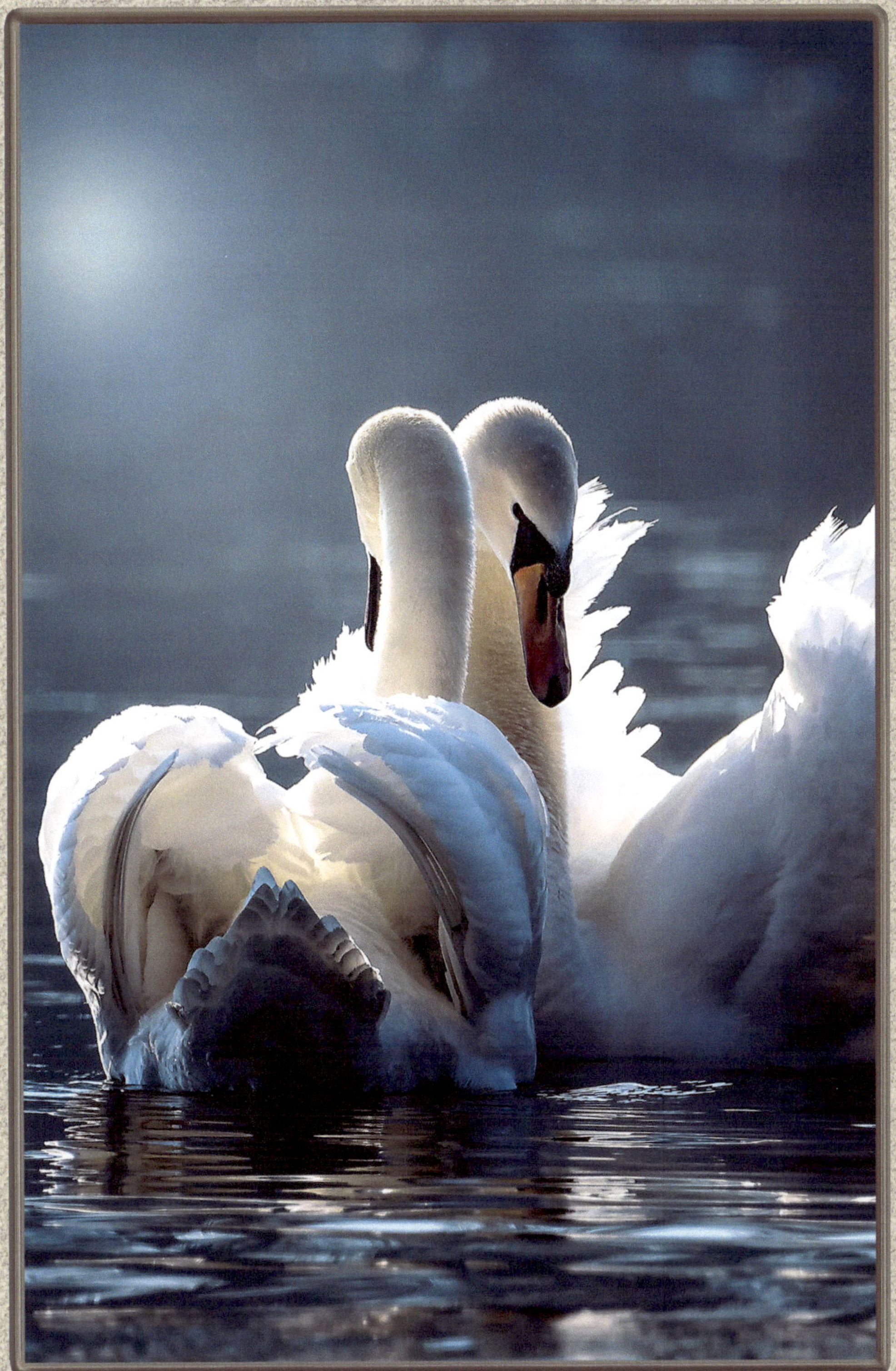

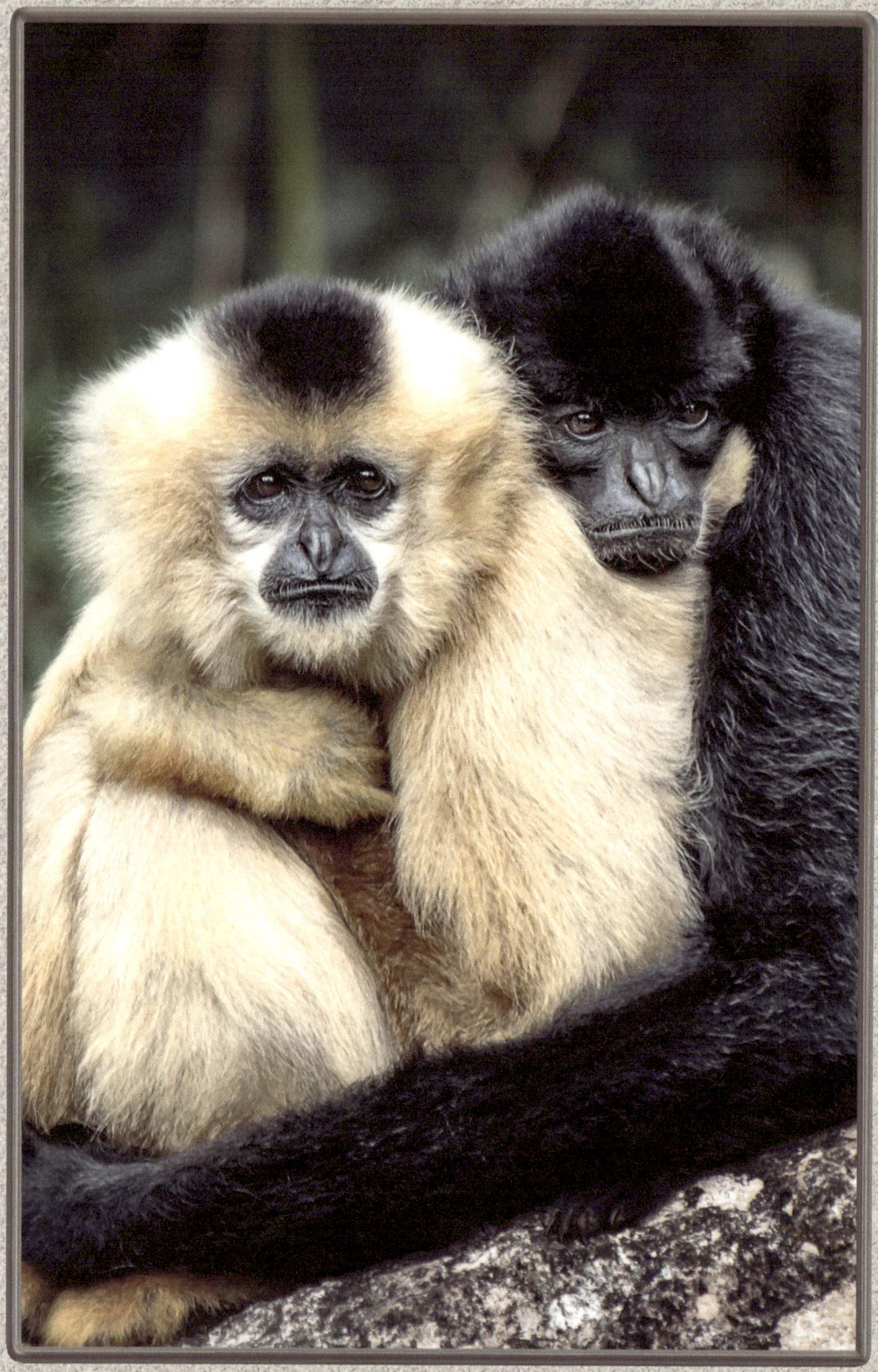

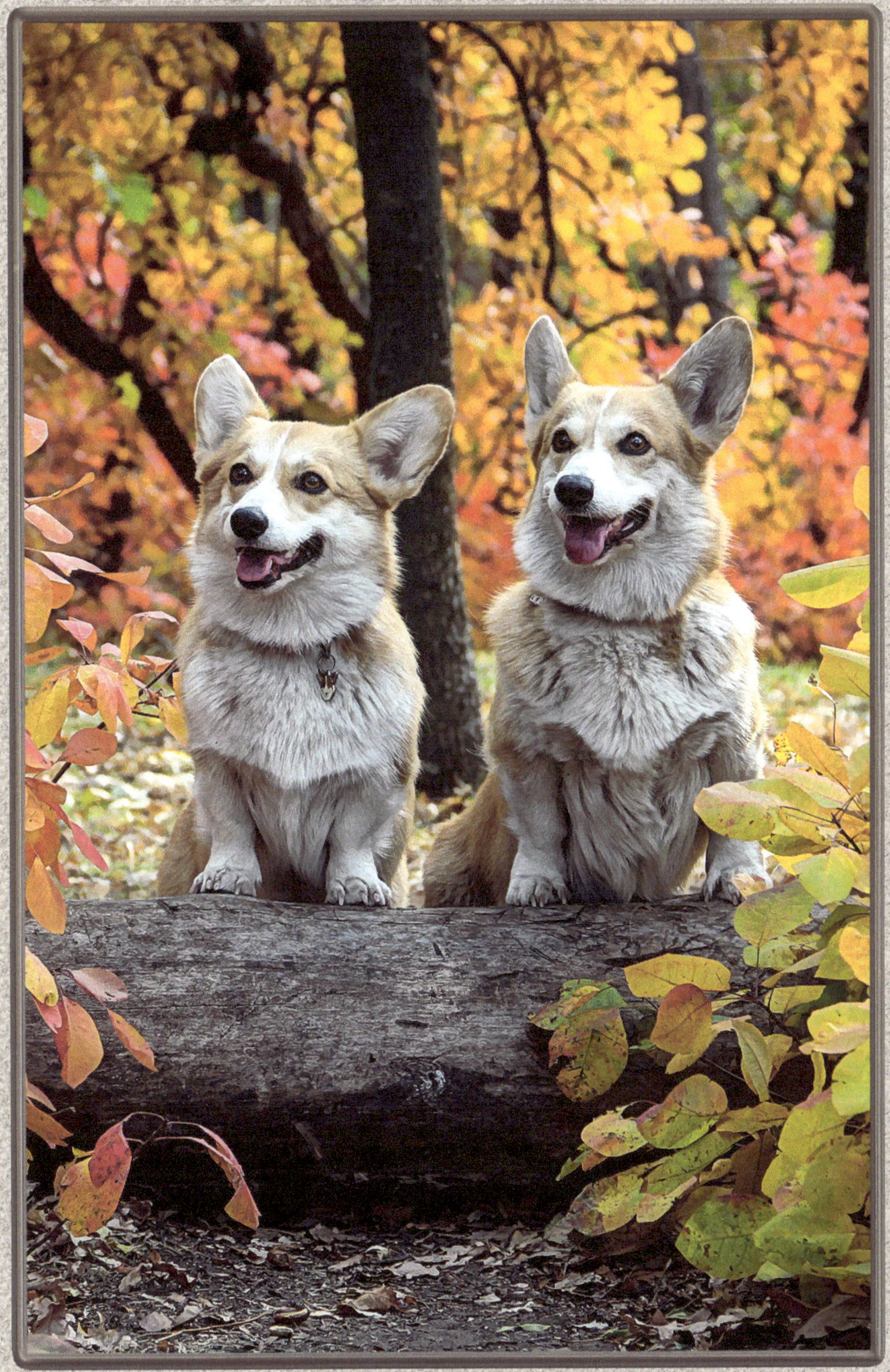

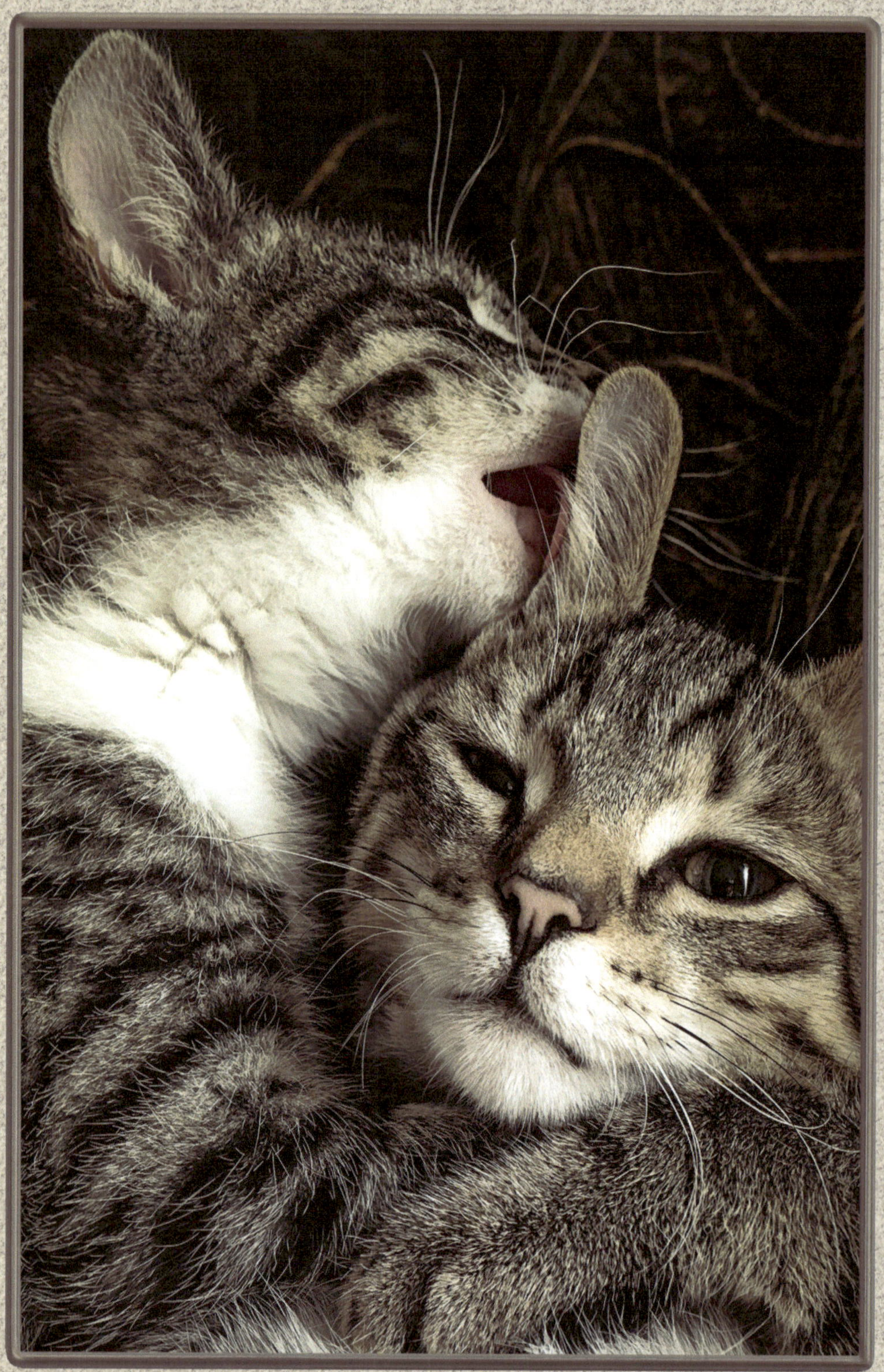

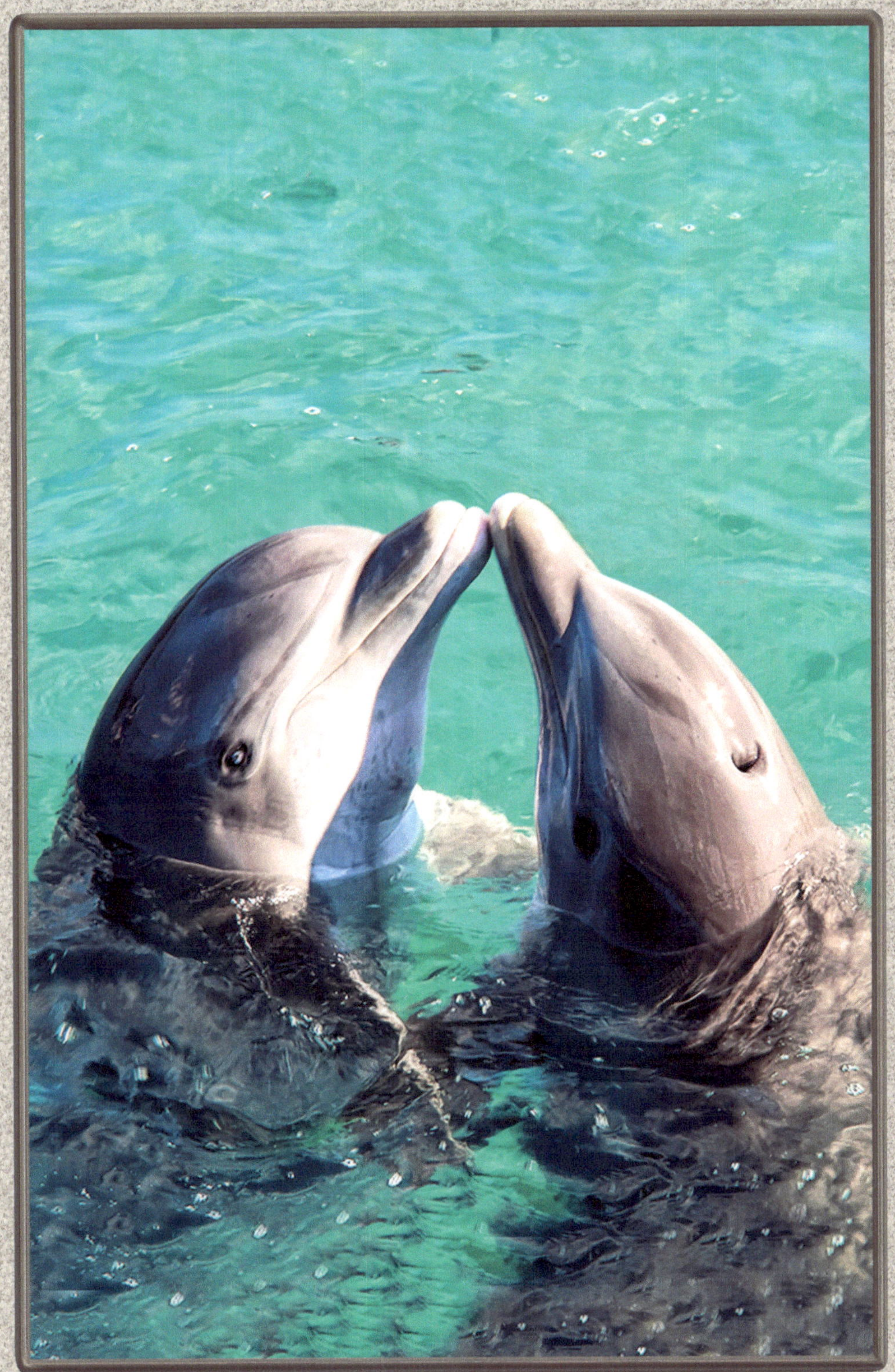

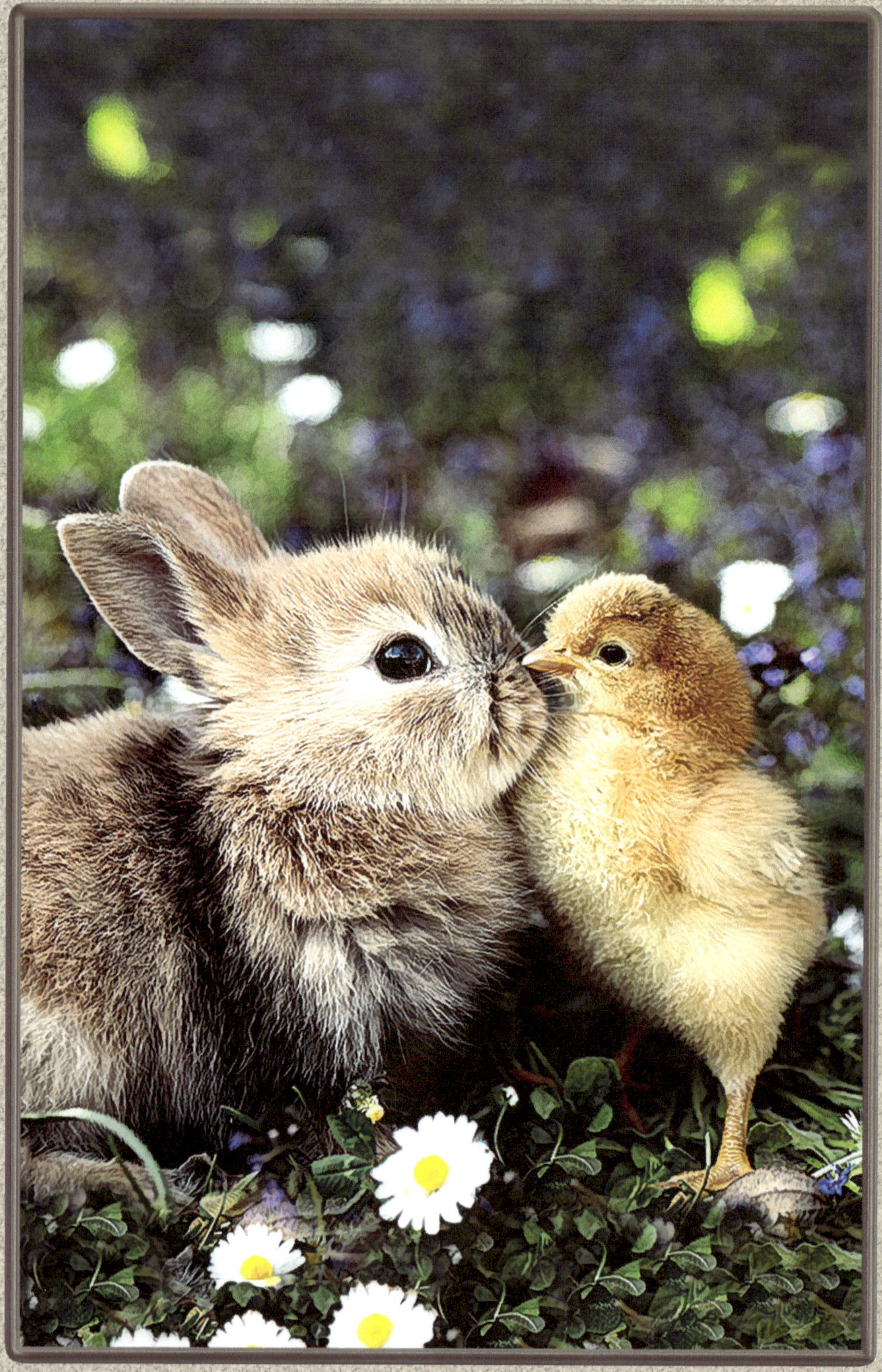

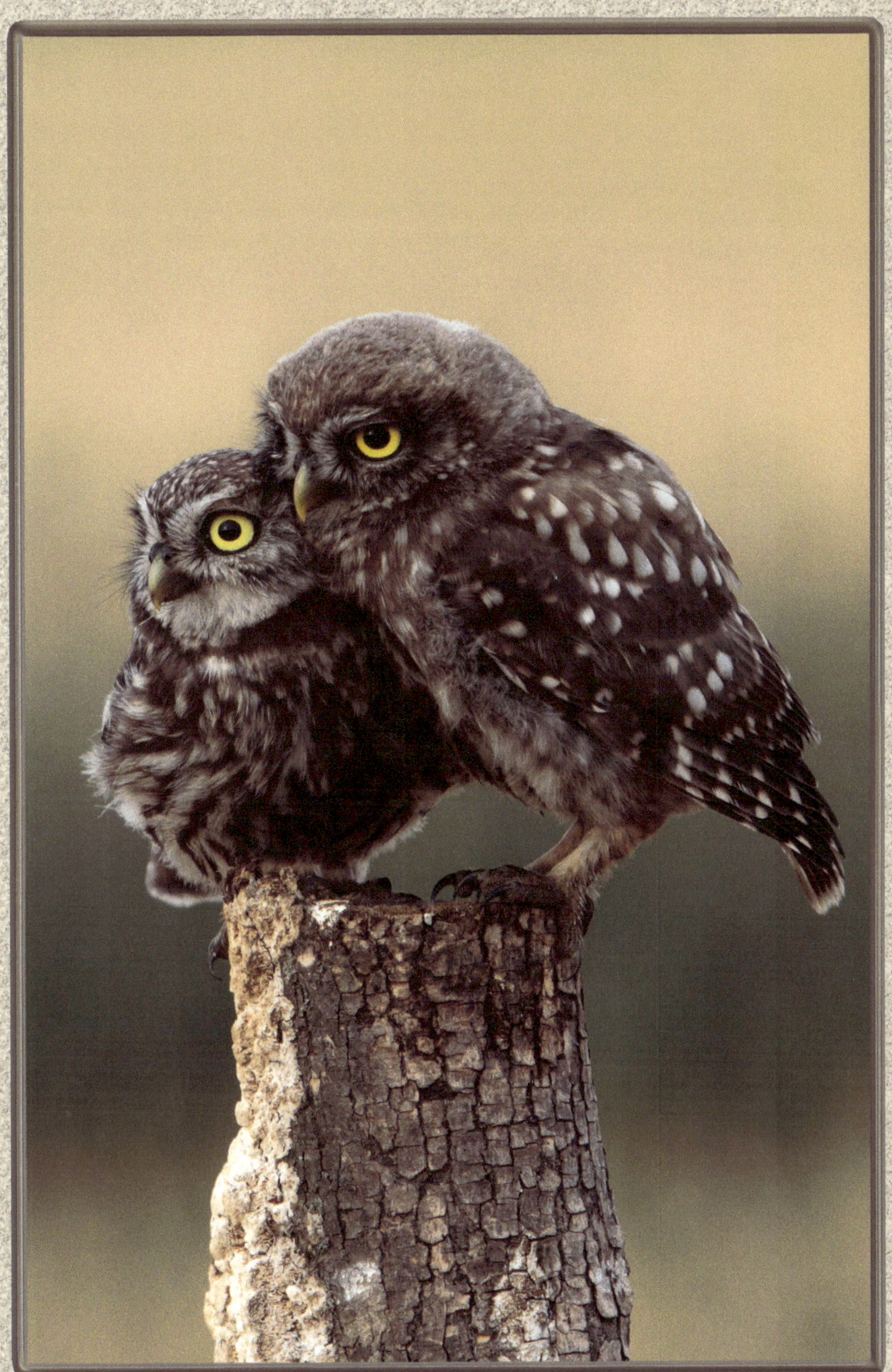

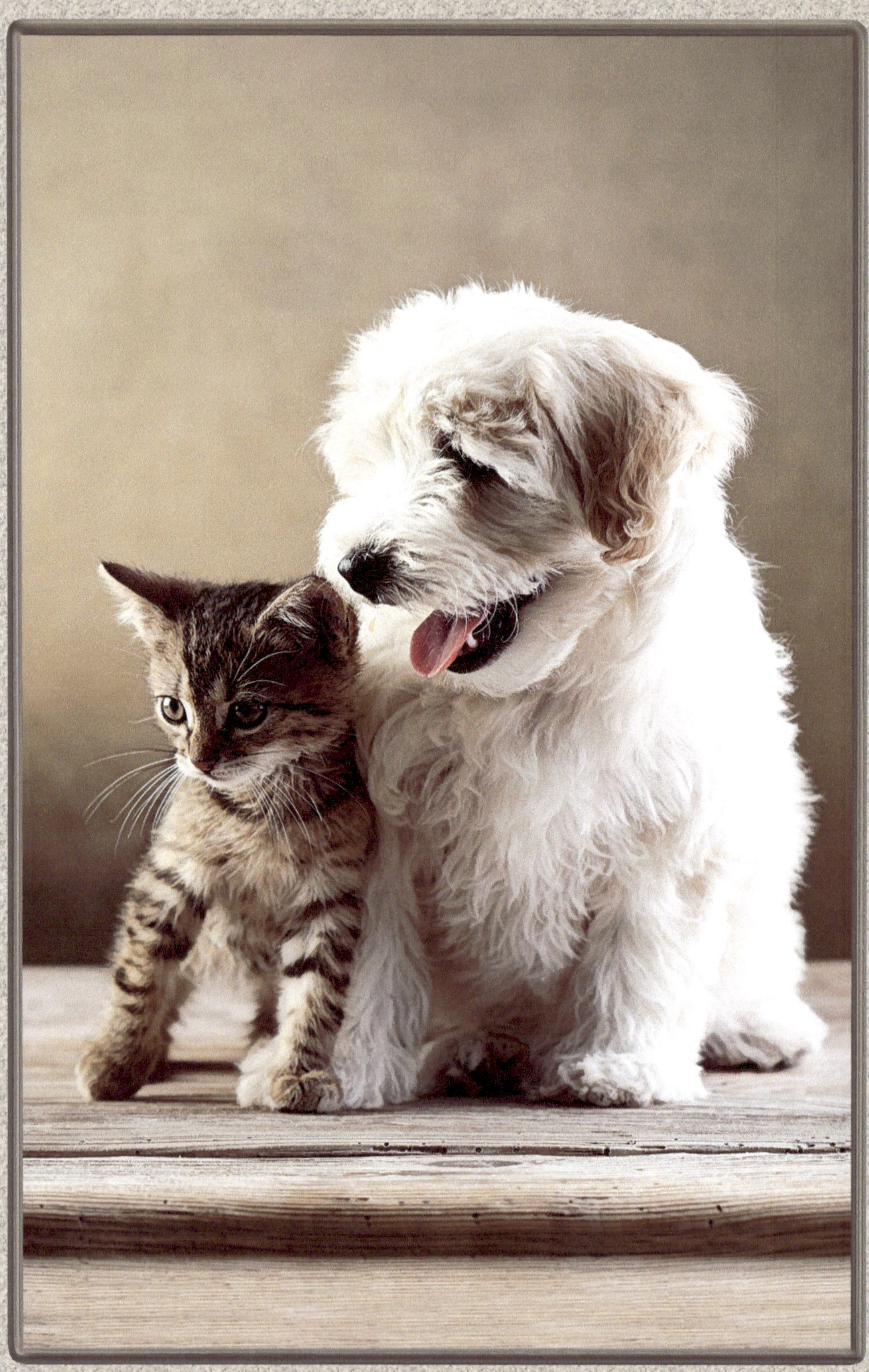

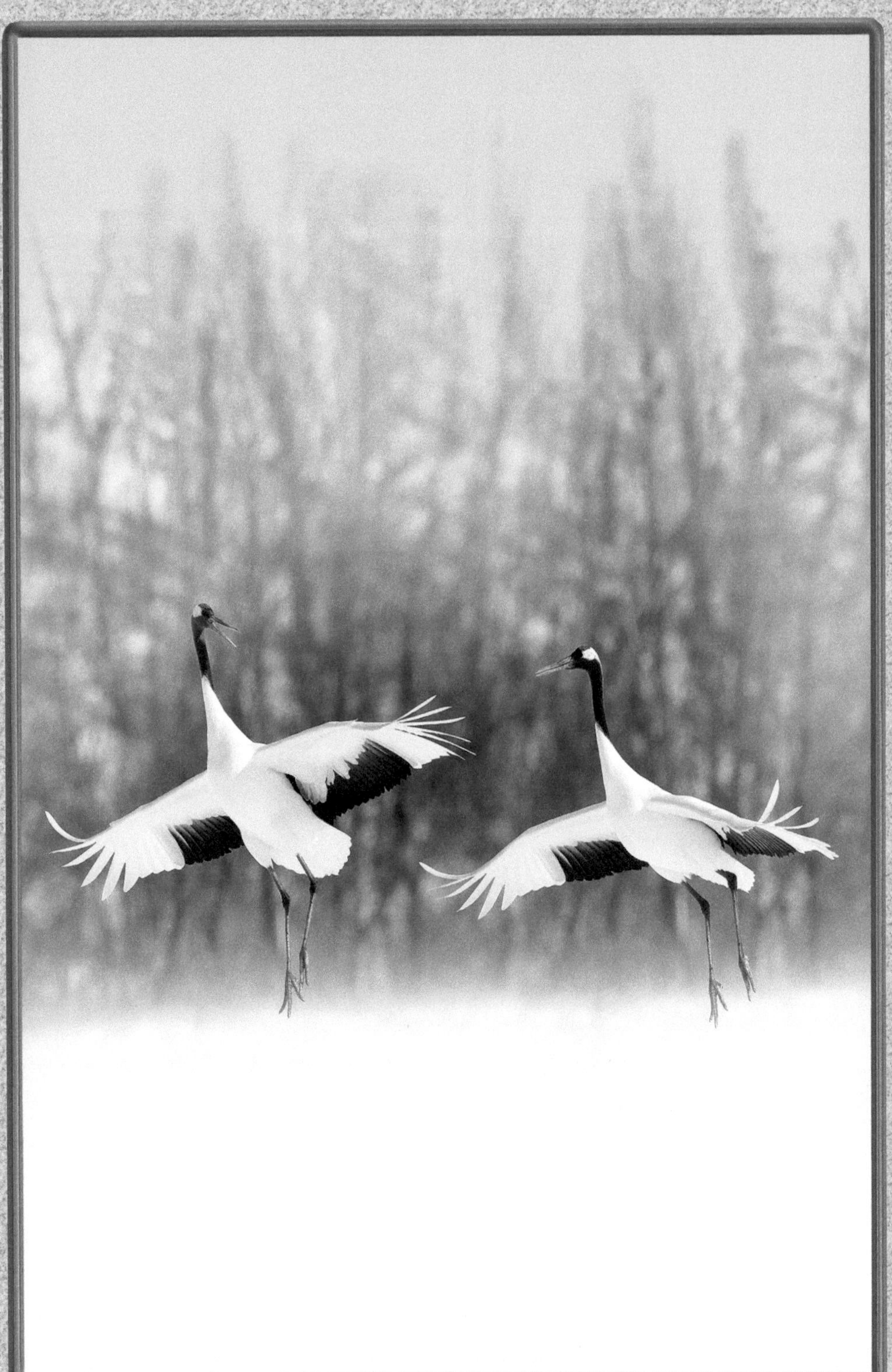

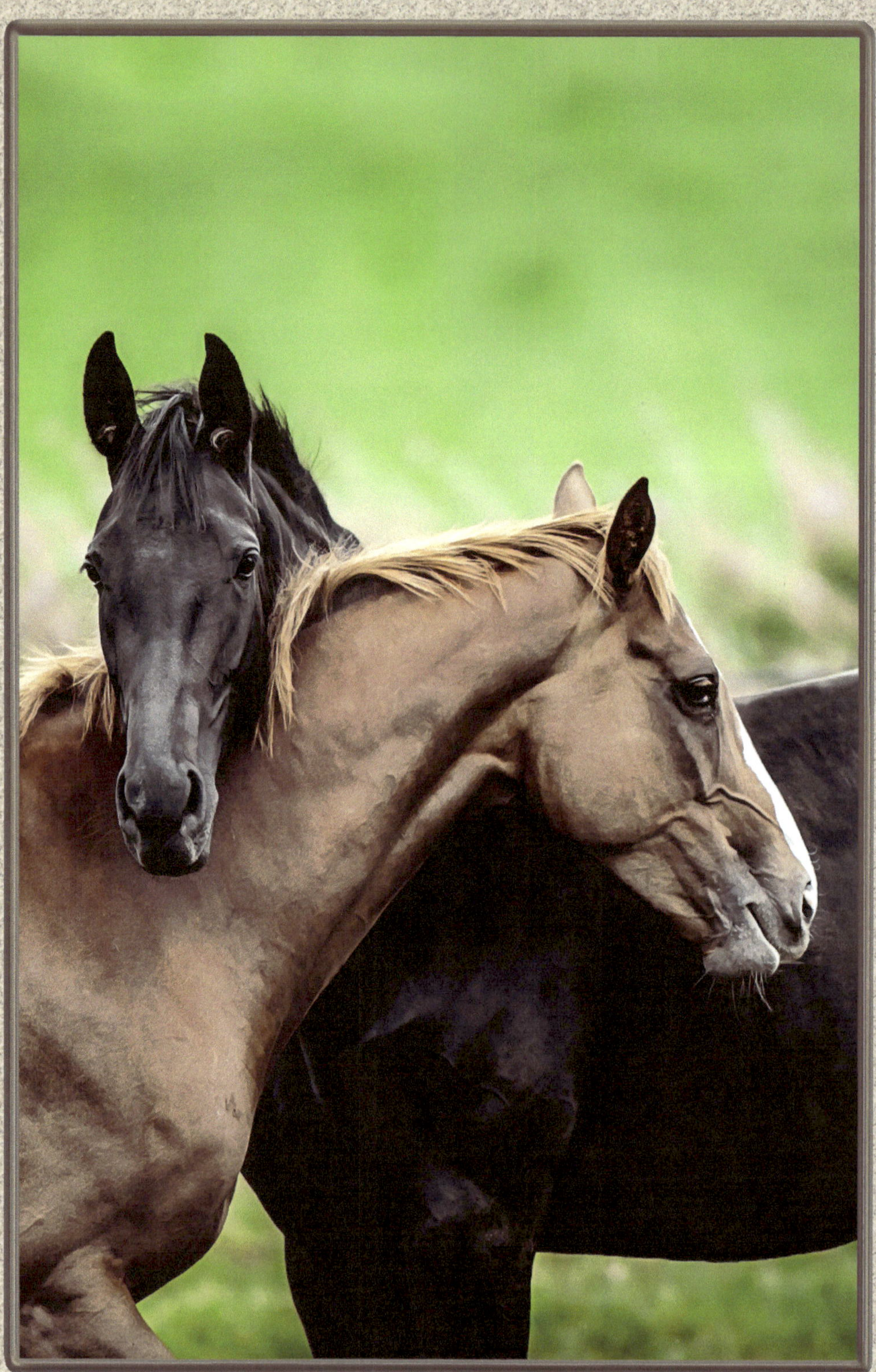

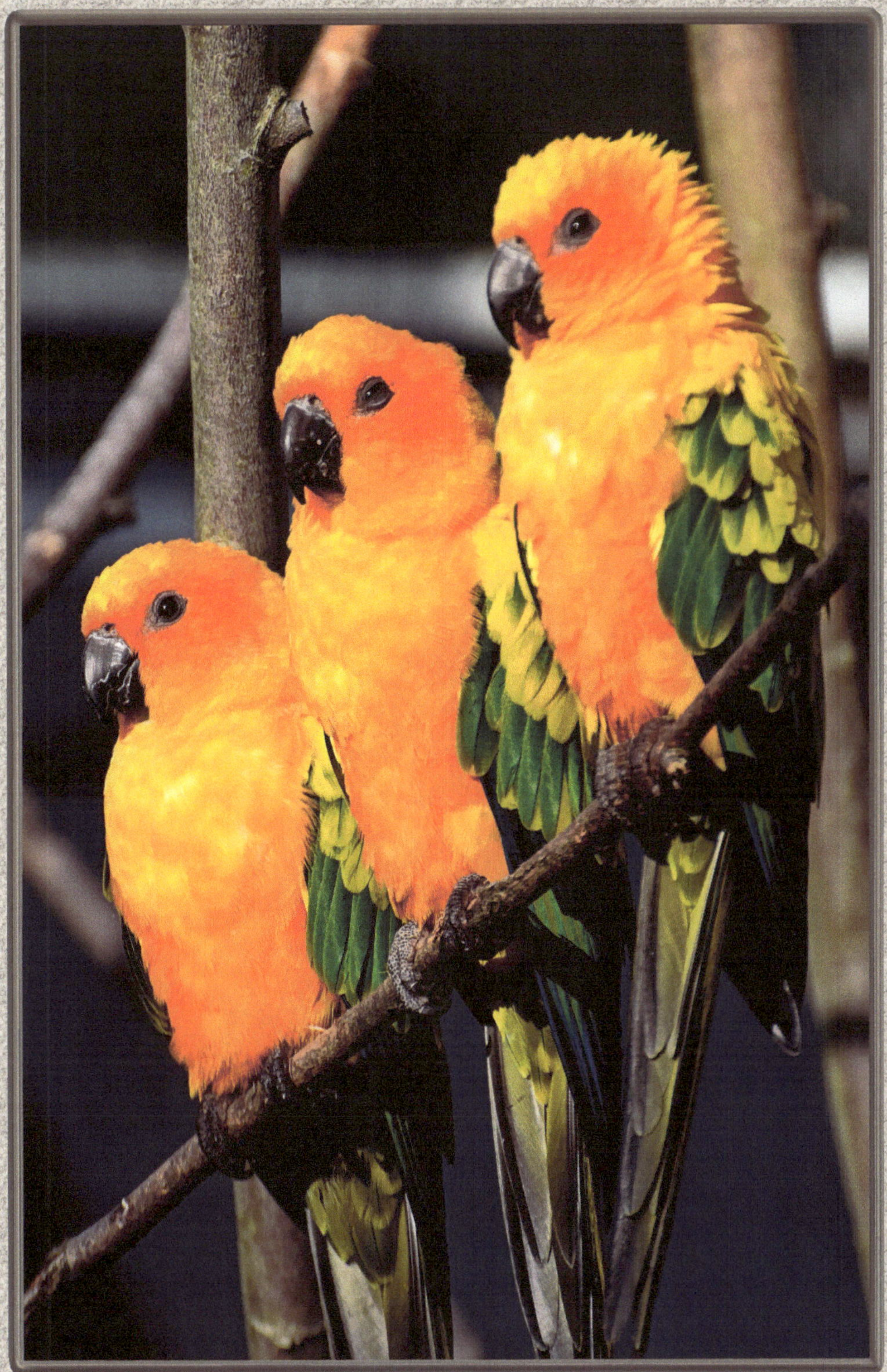

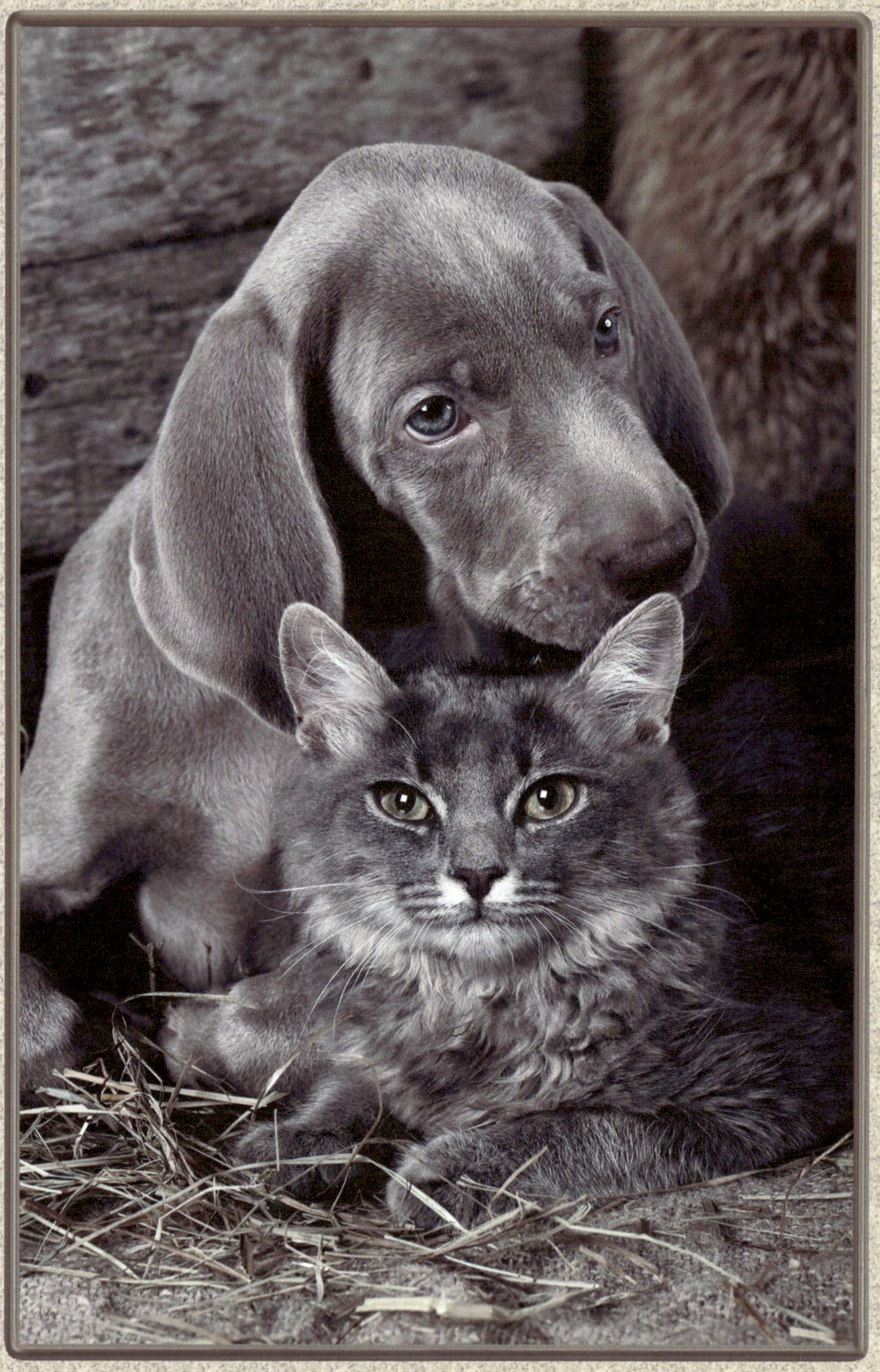

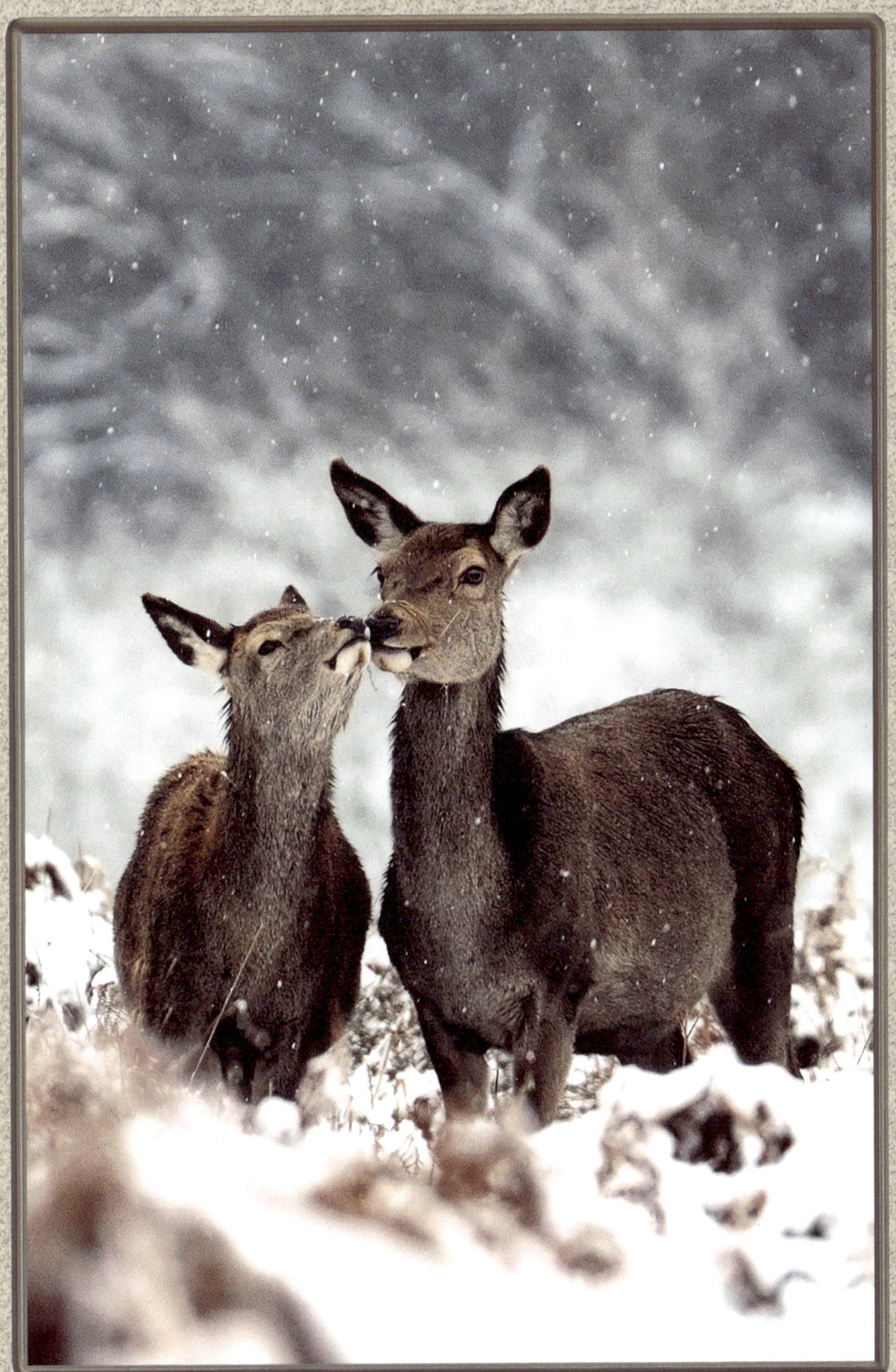

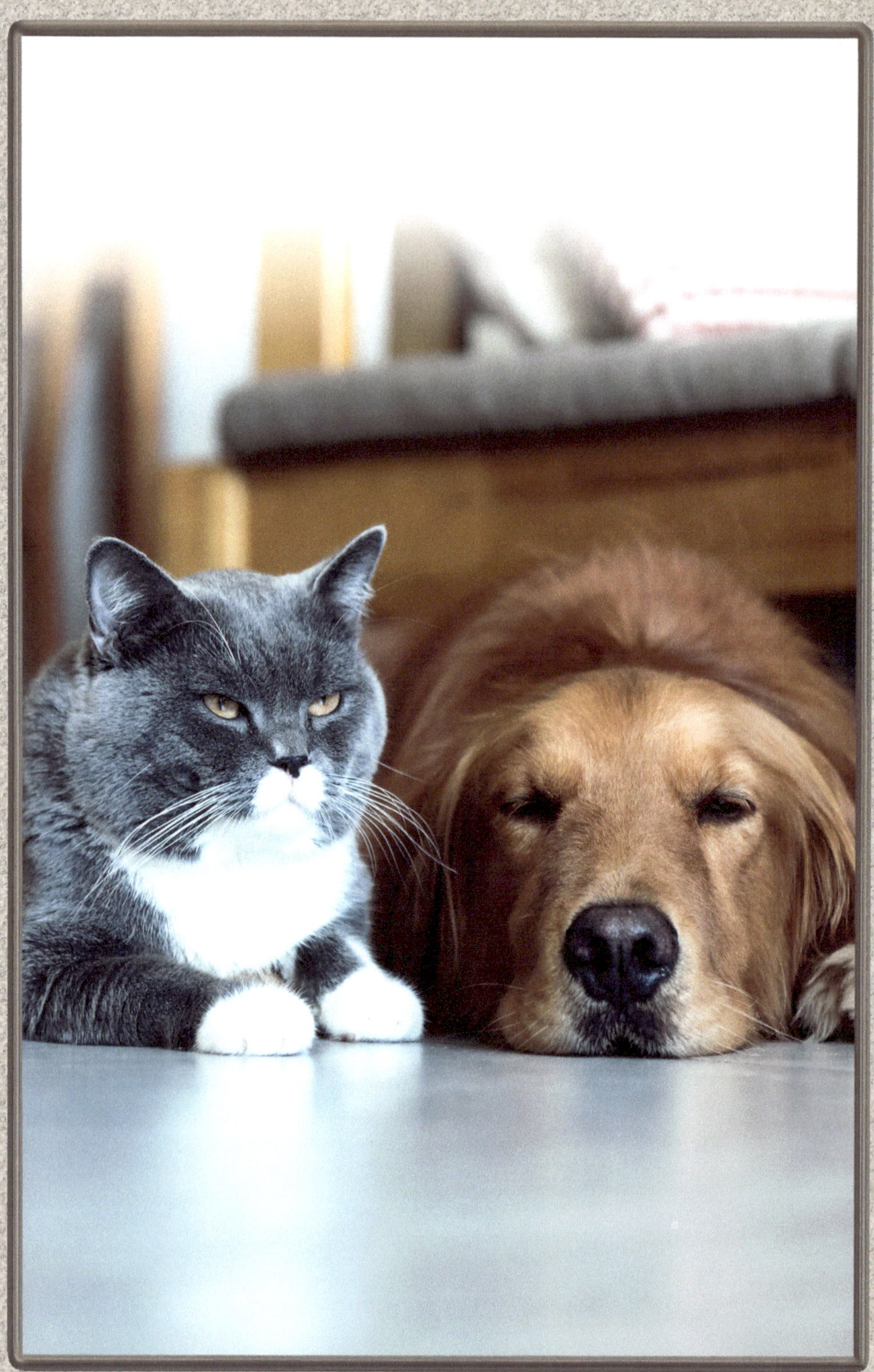

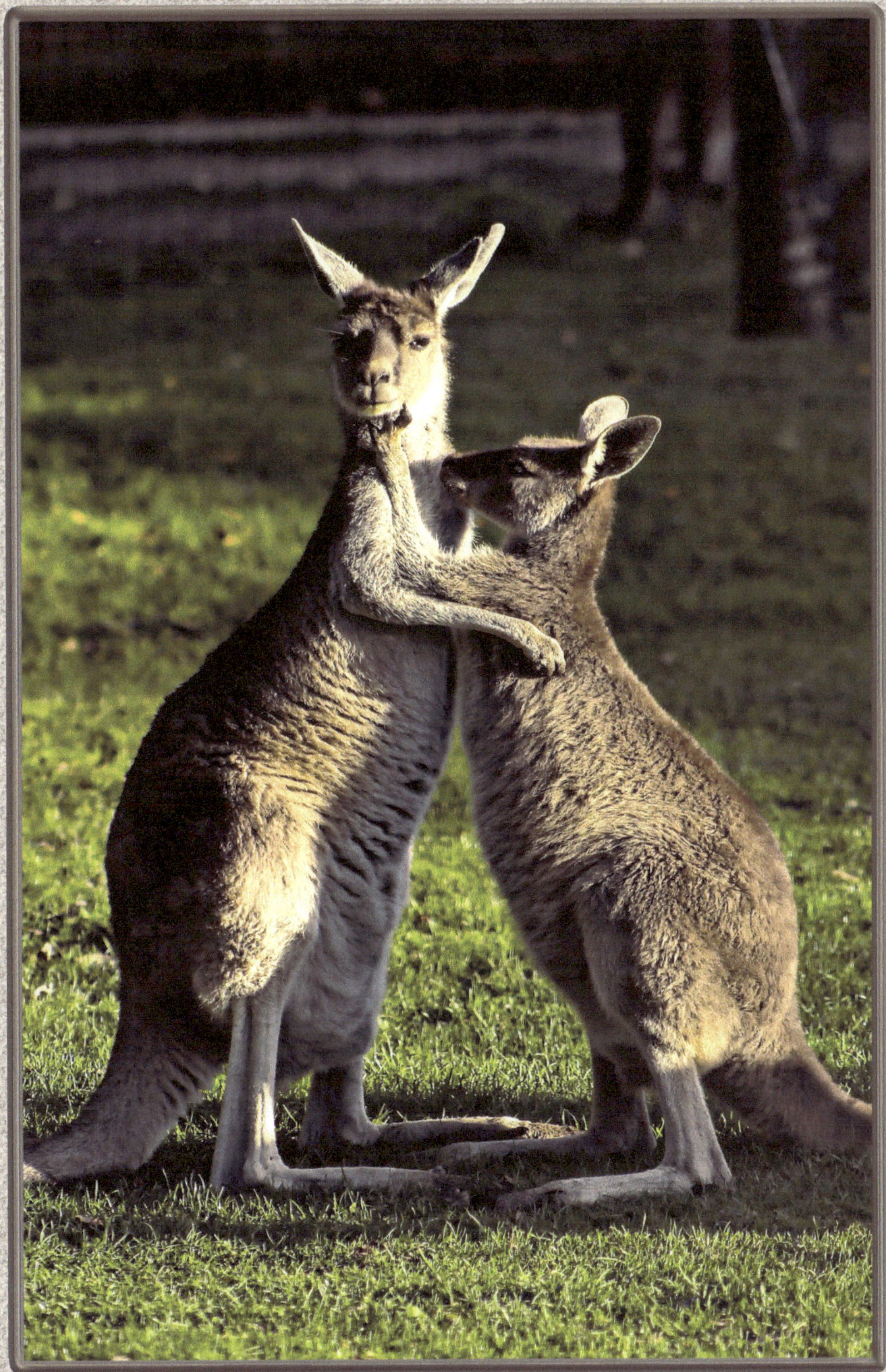

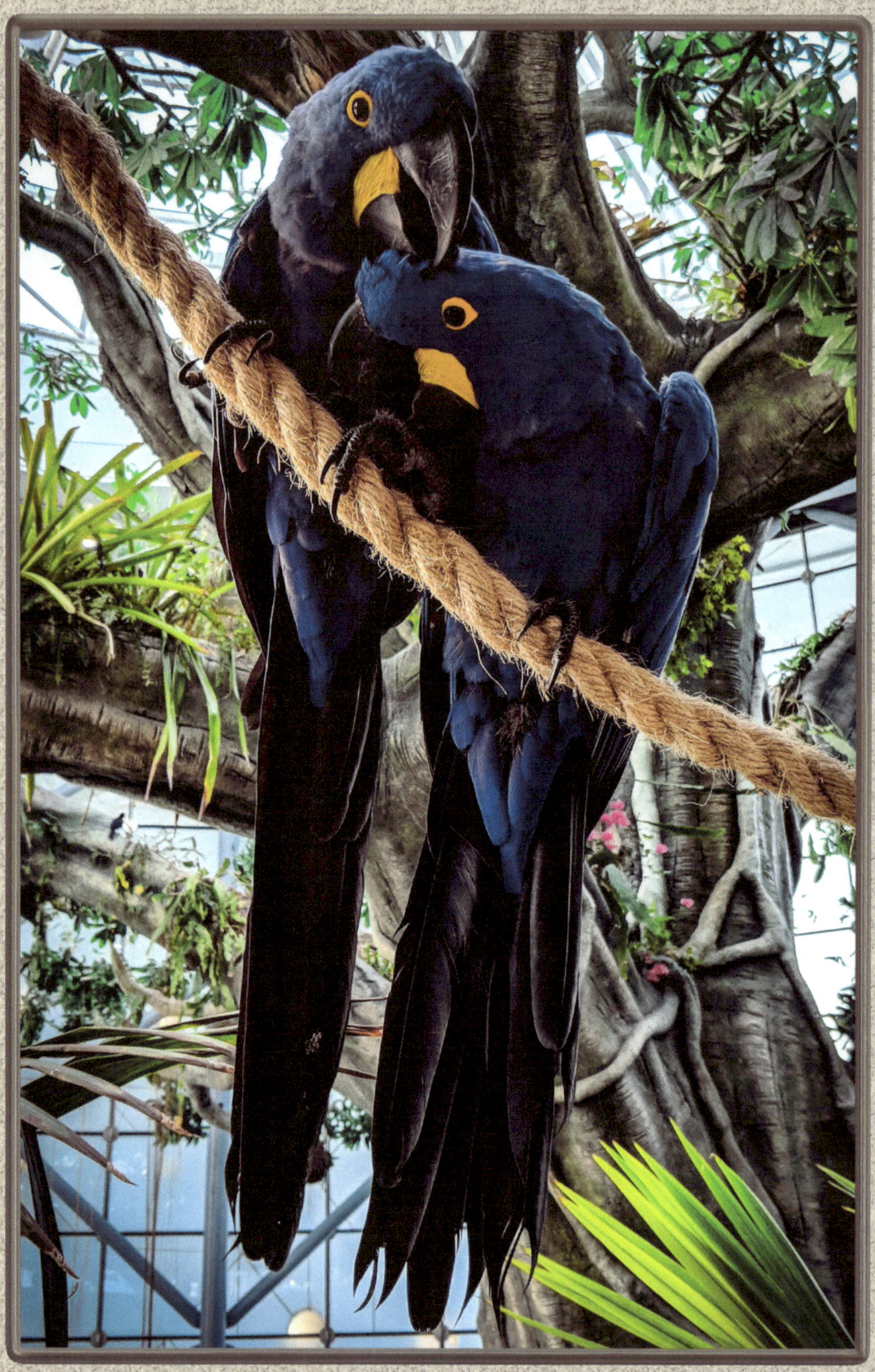

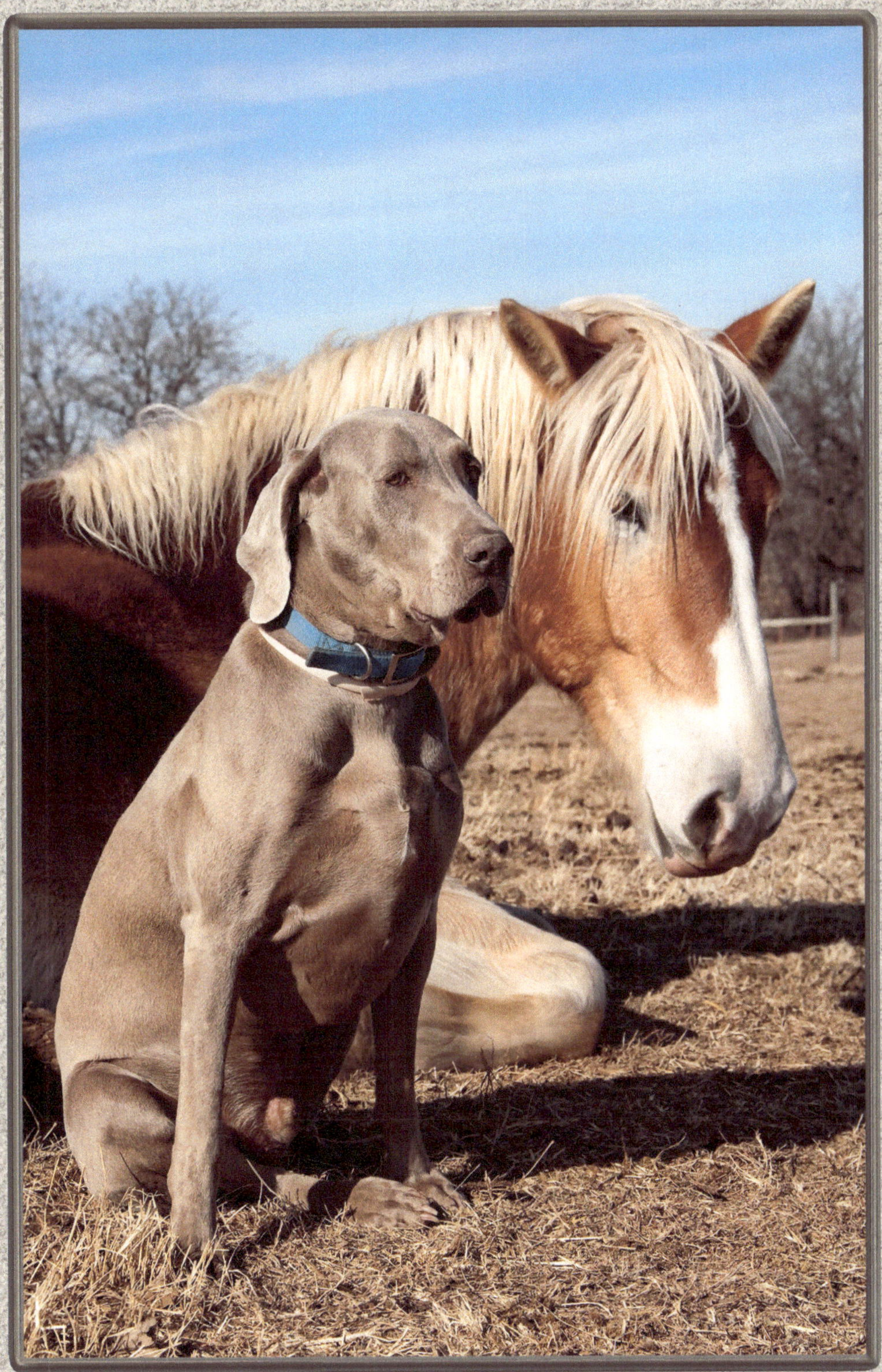

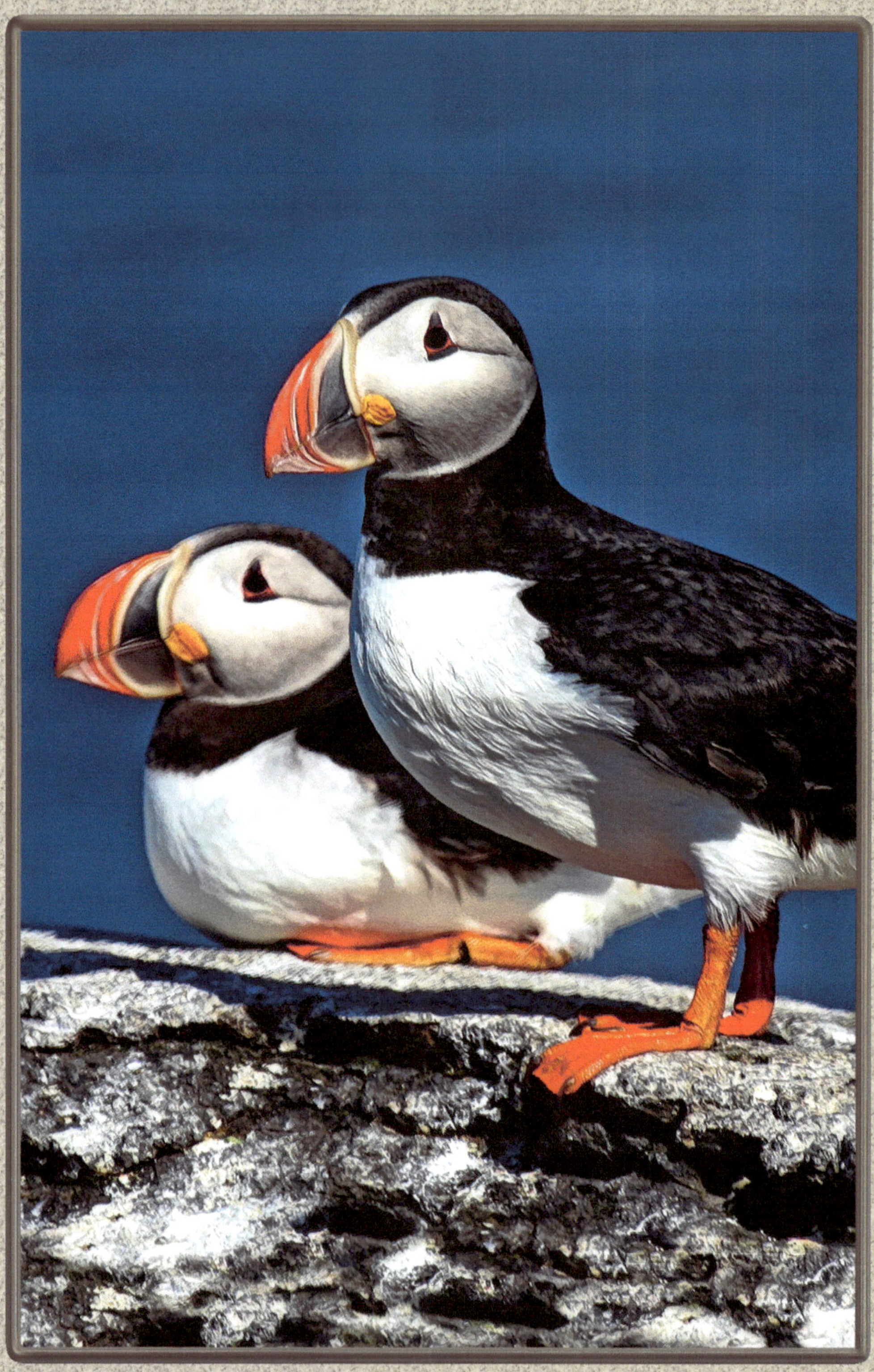

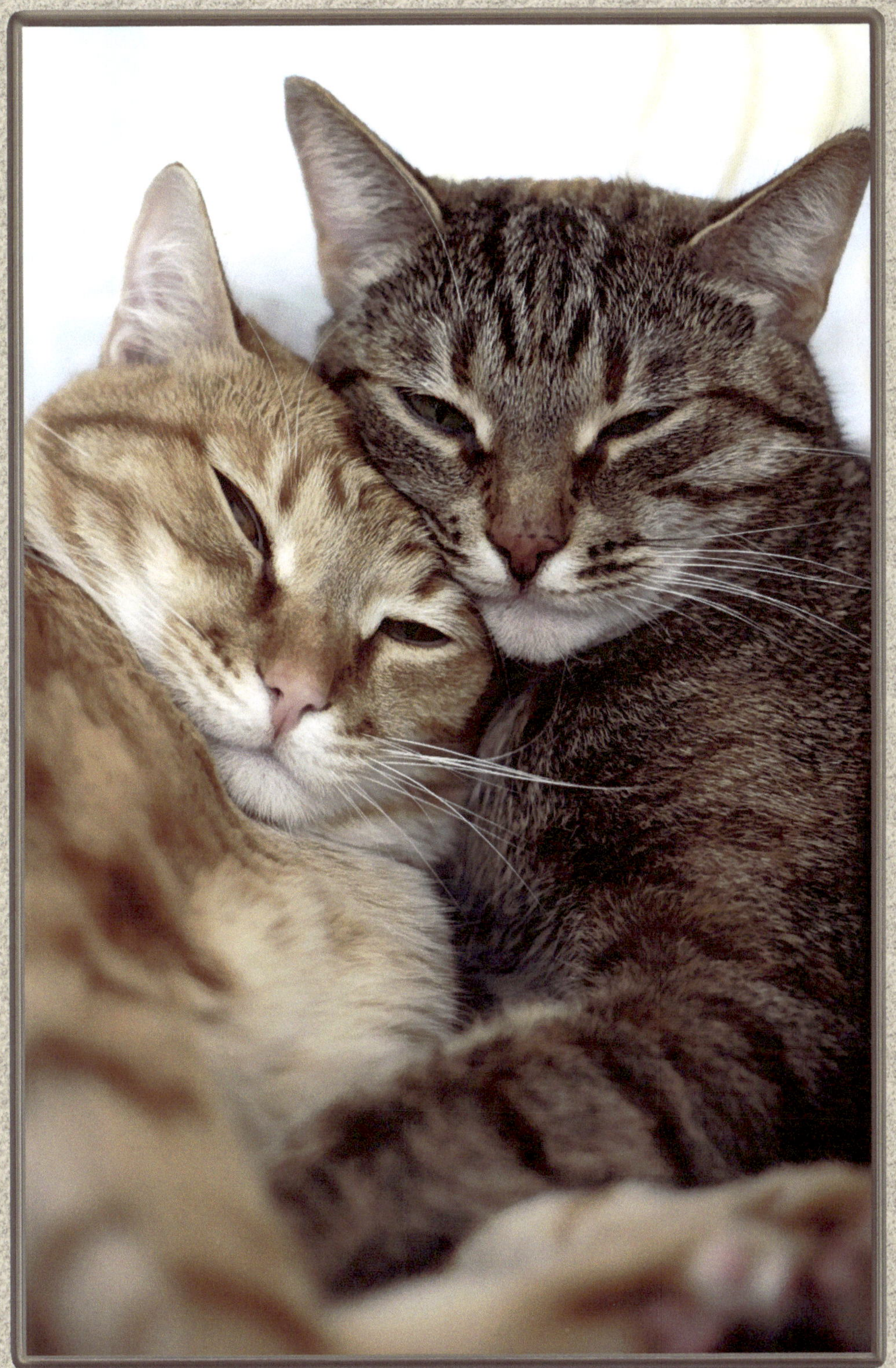

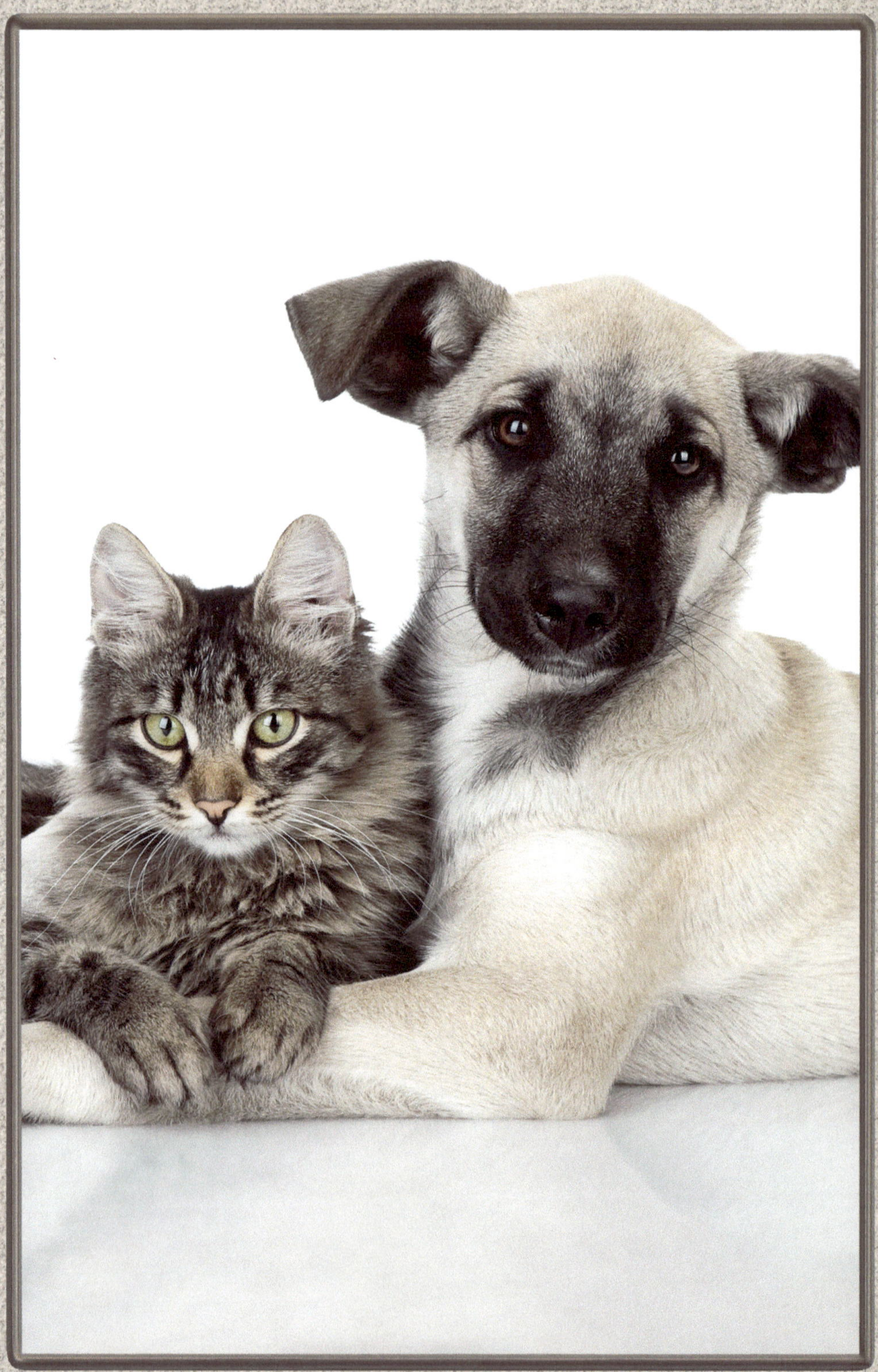

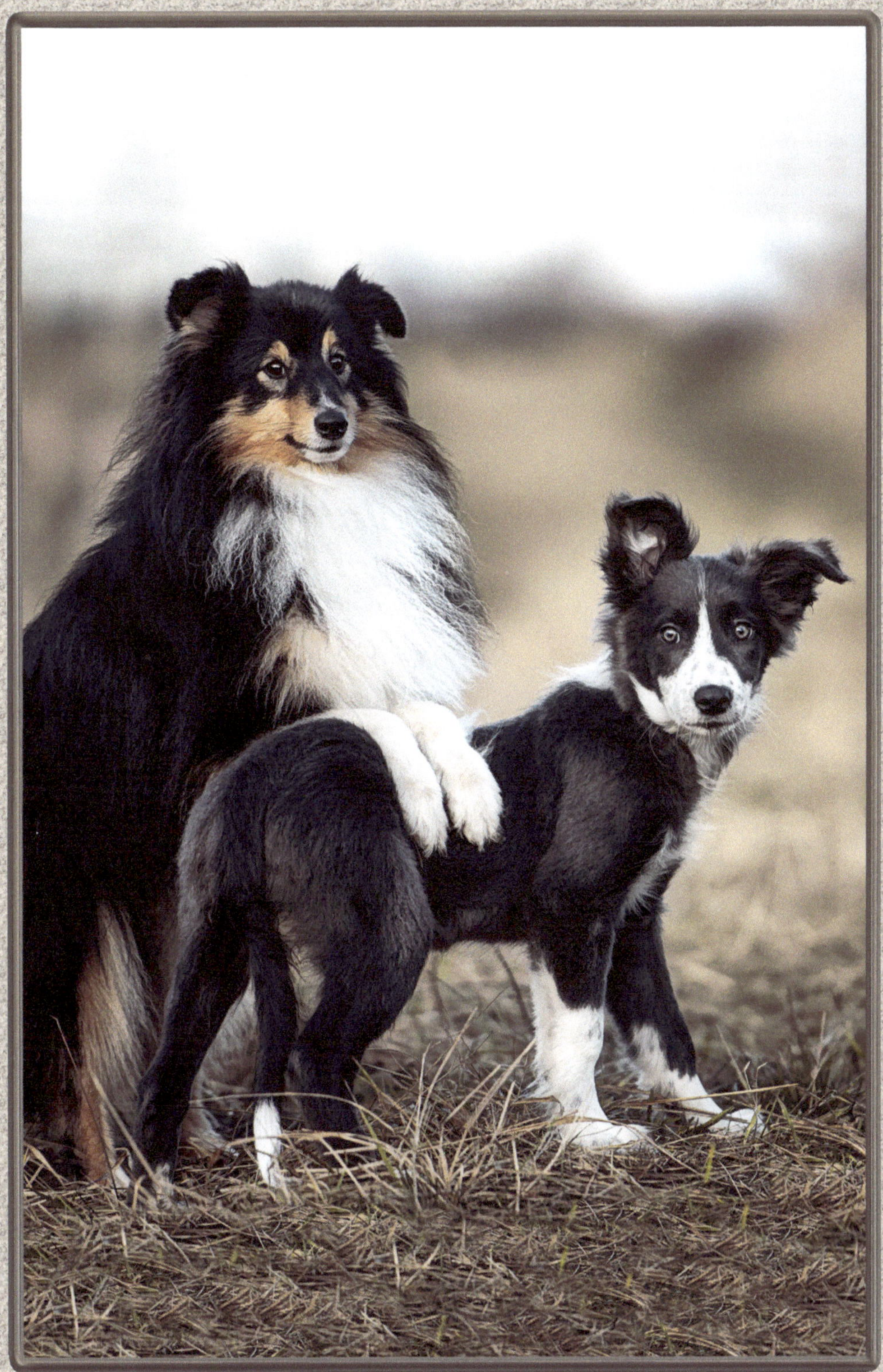

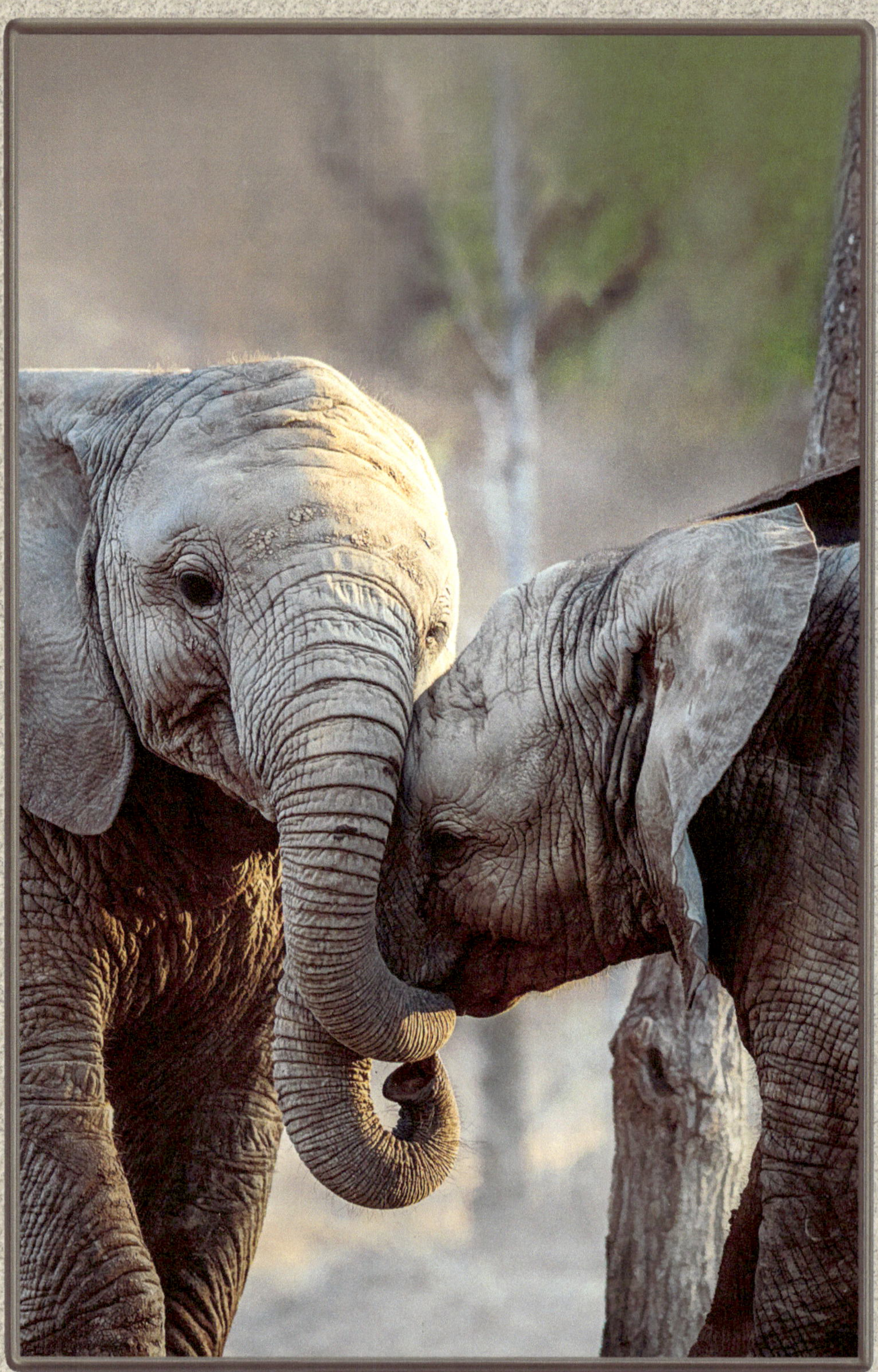

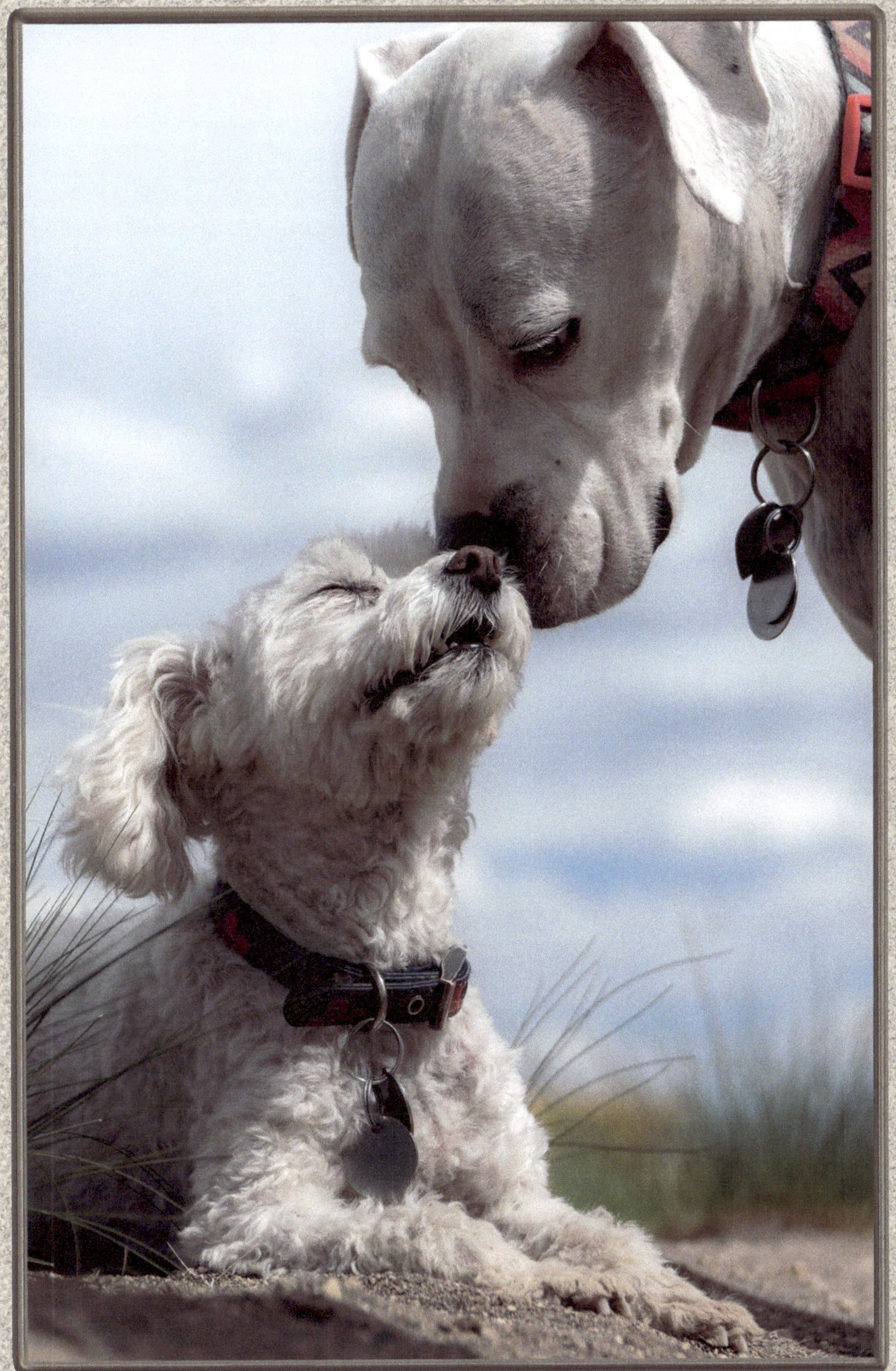

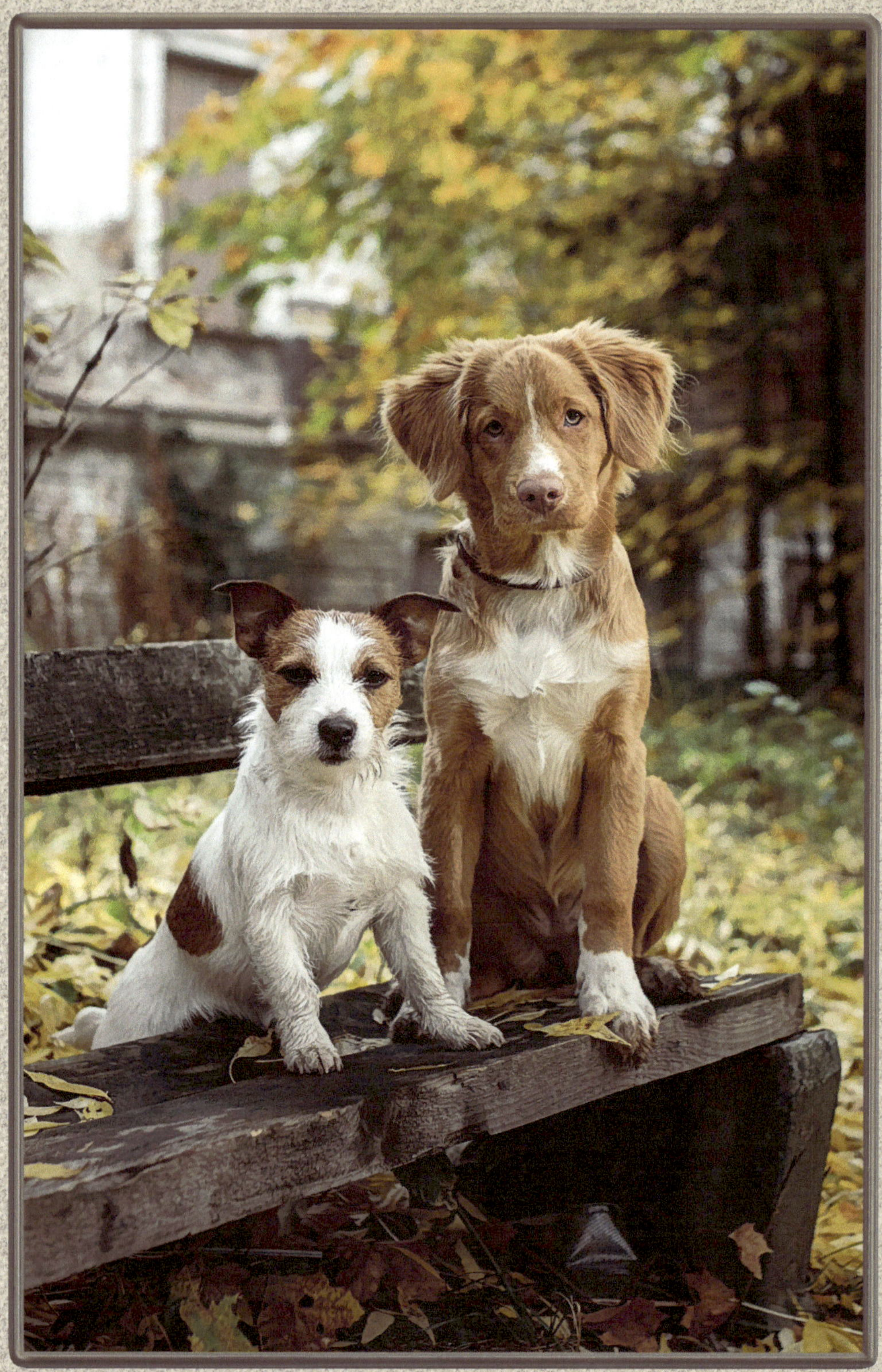

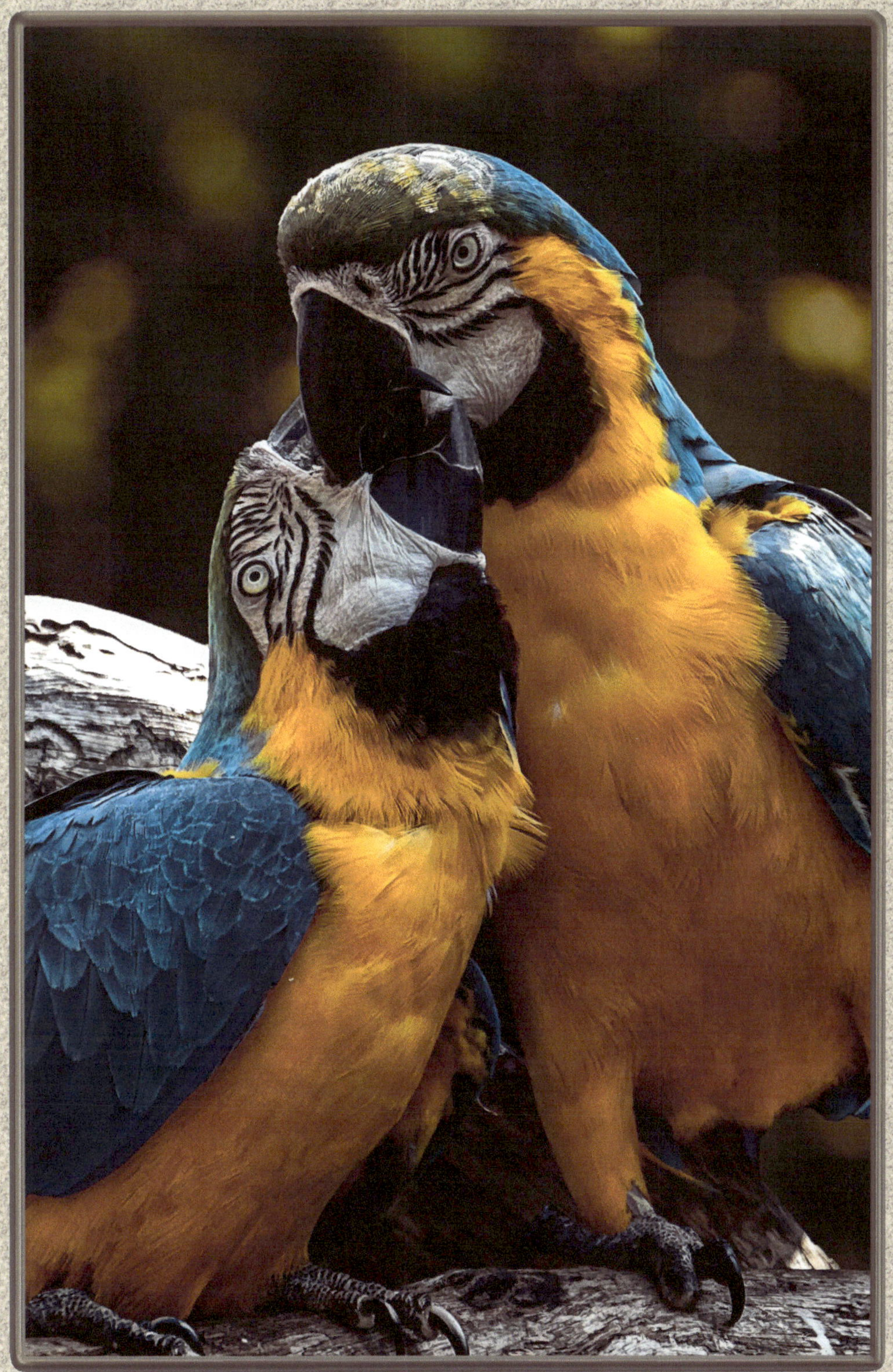

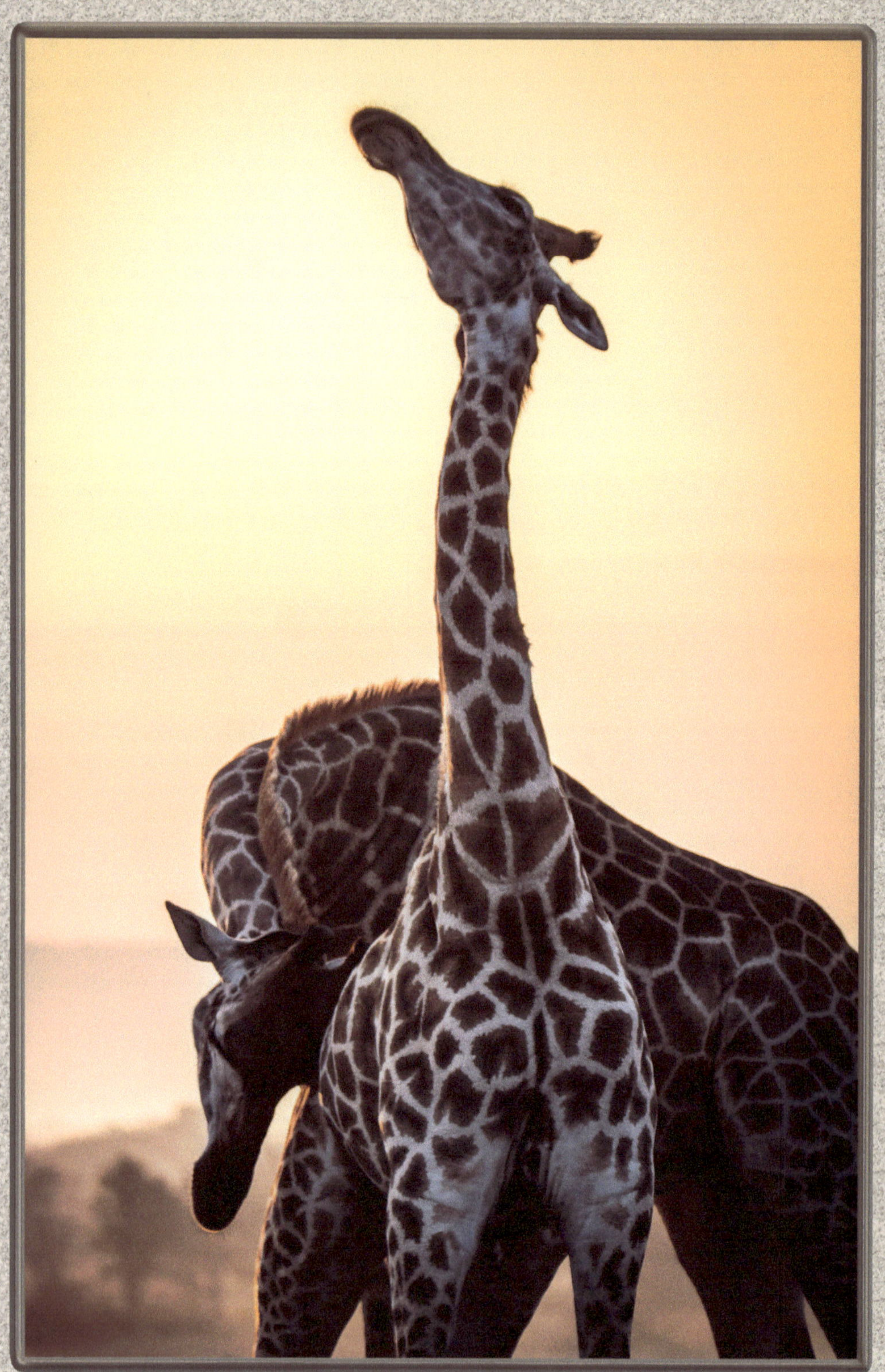

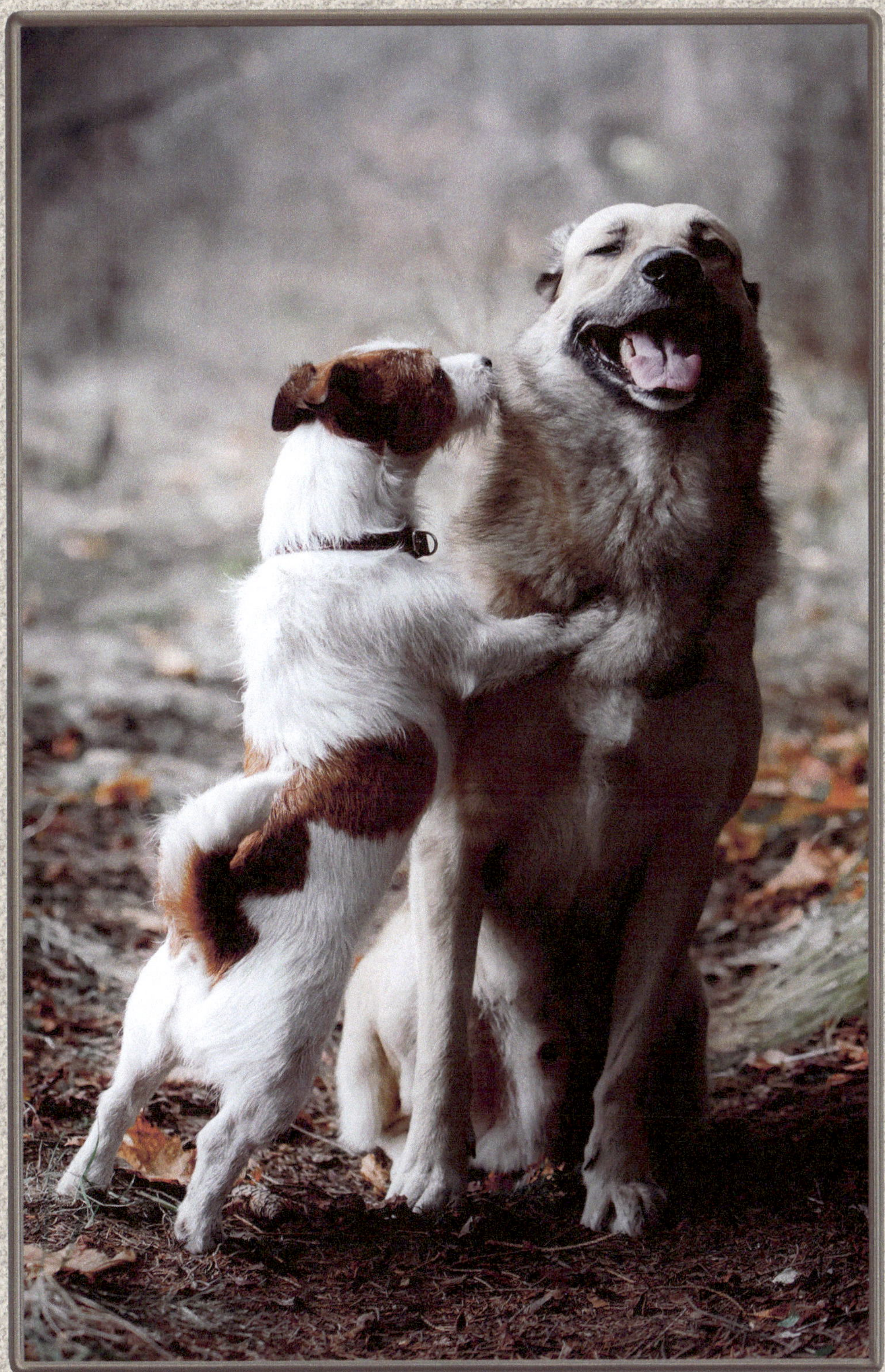

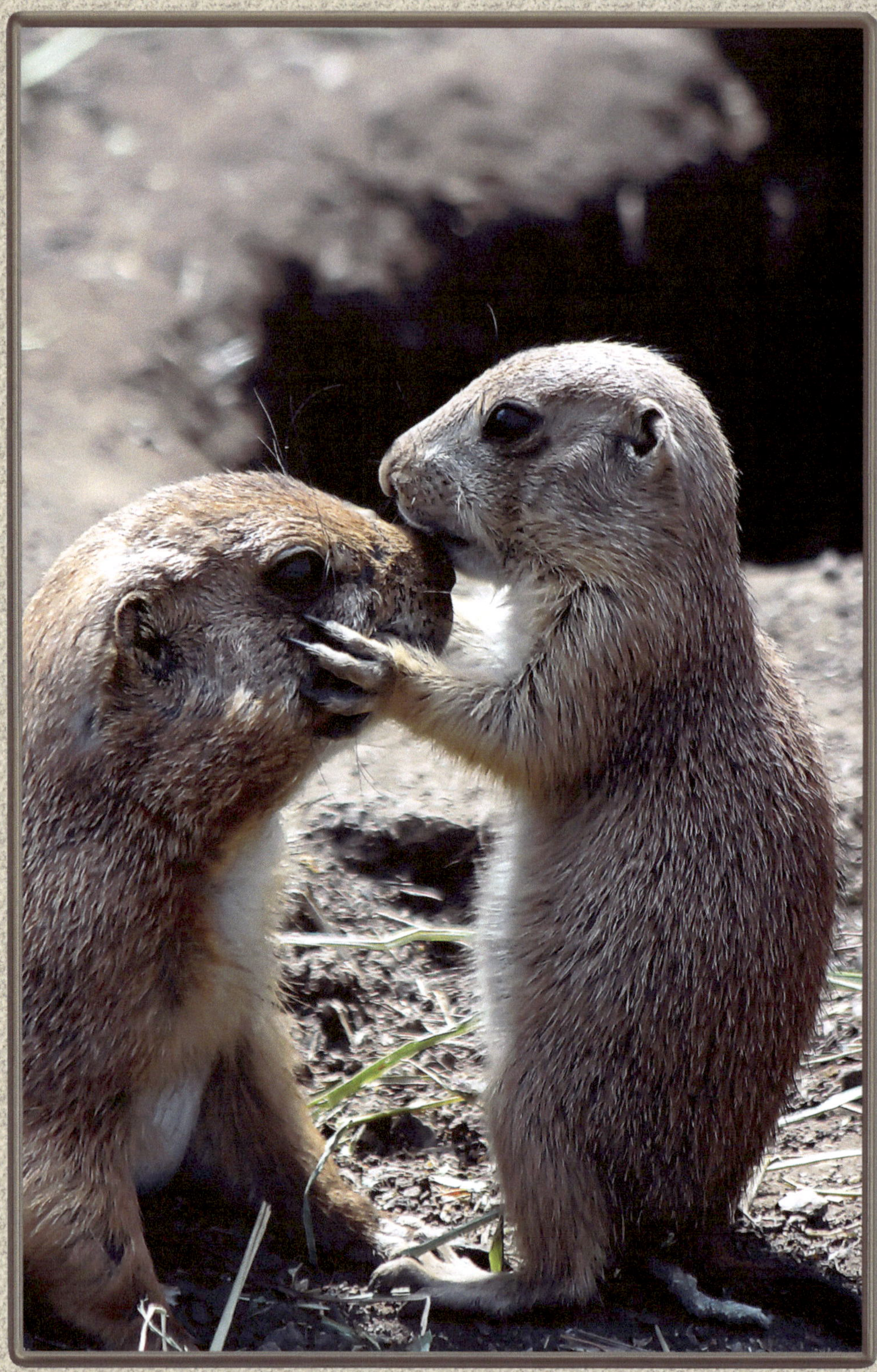

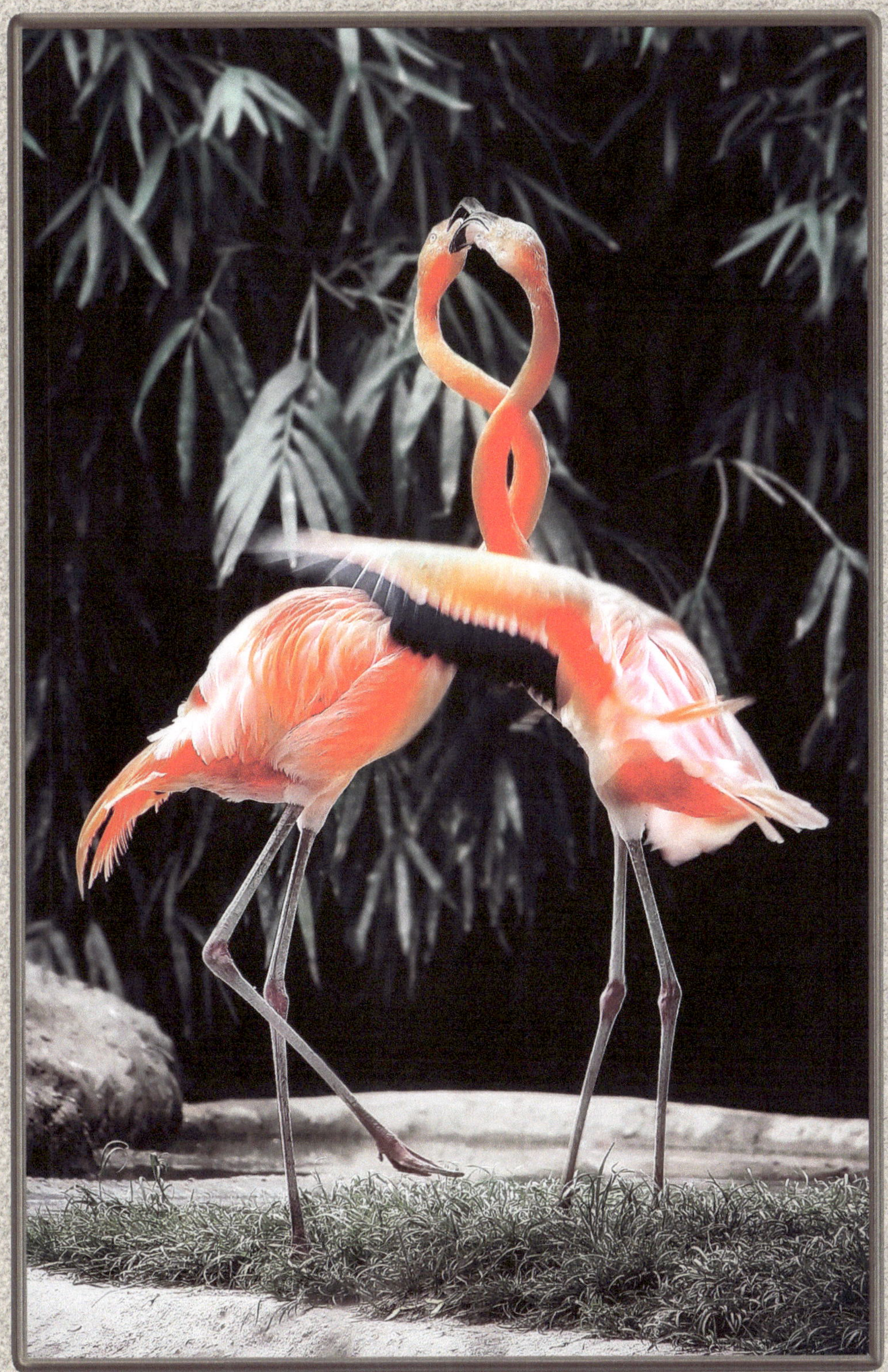